Complaining as a Sociocultural Activity

Complaining as a Sociocultural Activity

Examining How and Why in Korean Interaction

Kyung-Eun Yoon

LEXINGTON BOOKS
Lanham • Boulder • New York • London

Published by Lexington Books
An imprint of The Rowman & Littlefield Publishing Group, Inc.
4501 Forbes Boulevard, Suite 200, Lanham, Maryland 20706
www.rowman.com

6 Tinworth Street, London SE11 5AL, United Kingdom

Copyright © 2021 The Rowman & Littlefield Publishing Group, Inc.

All rights reserved. No part of this book may be reproduced in any form or by any electronic or mechanical means, including information storage and retrieval systems, without written permission from the publisher, except by a reviewer who may quote passages in a review.

British Library Cataloguing in Publication Information Available

Library of Congress Cataloging-in-Publication Data

Library of Congress Control Number: 2020945000

ISBN 978-1-7936-0470-5 (cloth)
ISBN 978-1-7936-0472-9 (pbk)
ISBN 978-1-7936-0471-2 (electronic)

Contents

List of Figures — vii

Transcription Conventions for Conversational Data — ix

Acknowledgments — xi

1 Introduction — 1

2 Formulating Complainability — 7

3 Linguistic Resources in Complaints — 39

4 Organization of Complaining Activity — 69

5 Social Organization in Complaining Activity — 113

6 Concluding Remarks — 145

Bibliography — 149

Index — 155

About the Author — 157

List of Figures

Figure 3.1　Regular Rising Intonation versus Later Upward Intonation　60
Figure 3.2　Variations of Later Upward Intonation　60
Figure 4.1　Complaining Activity Organized through Response Cries　73

Transcription Conventions for Conversational Data

(Adapted from Ochs et al. 1996, 461–465)

[	The point at which overlapping talk starts
]	The point at which overlapping talk ends
=	If the two lines connected by the equal signs are produced: (1) by the same speaker, the continuous talk is broken up to accommodate the placement of overlapping talk; (2) if they are produced by different speakers, the second follows the first with no discernable silence between them (i.e., "latched" to it).
(0.5)	The length of silence in tenths of a second
(.)	Micro-pause
word	Some form of stress or emphasis, either by increased loudness or higher pitch
WOrd	Especially loud talk
°word°	A passage of talk quieter than the surrounding talk
:::	The prolongation or stretching of the sound just preceding them
.	Falling, or final intonation
?	Rising intonation
,	Half-rising intonation
¿	Rising stronger than a comma but weaker than a question mark
_:	Inflected falling intonation contour
:̣	Inflected rising intonation contour
↑↑	A passage of talk with higher pitch than the surrounding talk
> <	Increase in tempo, as in a rush-through
< >	Markedly slow talk
<	"Jump-started," i.e., starting with a rush
--	A cut-off or self-interruption (modified to be distinguished from the morpheme boundary marker, -)
hhh	Audible outbreath
.hh	Audible inbreath
(hh)	Laughter within a word
(word)	Uncertainty of hearing on the transcriber's part
( )	Something being said, but no hearing achieved
(( ))	Transcriber's remark

Acknowledgments

This book is a substantially revised version of my dissertation titled *Complaint Talk in Korean Conversation* (2006). An earlier version of section 3.2.2 in this book appeared in *Japanese/Korean Linguistics*, Vol. 14, edited by Timothy Vance and Kimberly Jones (CSLI, 2006). Since it has been a long time after completing the dissertation, I have updated the analysis with more recent data. In so doing, I also expanded the scope from ordinary conversation among family and friends to various other contexts including online postings and formal complaints. The scope of analysis has been expanded from direct complaints to indirect complaints about non-present third parties as well.

This book could not have been written without the support, encouragement, and help of a great many people. I am indebted to Makoto Hayashi for helping me lay the important groundwork as my dissertation director. He introduced me to fascinating views on the intertwined relationship between grammar and interaction. I would also like to express my deep appreciation to Irene Koshik, who introduced me to the amazing world of conversation analysis (CA). Learning the CA discipline has been the basis of my analysis on how social actions are carried out through language use.

Next, my sincere thanks goes to Mary Shin Kim who carefully read chapters of this manuscript and provided helpful comments and suggestions. I am also deeply grateful to my friend, Patricia Moon, for her help with proofreading, wonderful comments, and supportive conversations with me. I must extend my thanks to all of the anonymous participants in my data.

Lastly, but certainly not least, I am truly grateful to my husband and daughter for their never-ending love and support. My husband provided not only incredible mental support and encouragement but also a tremendous amount of practical help at many stages of this project, from collecting data and typing the everlasting transcripts to changing the bibliography style for this book. My daughter has been the most joyous support in my life. I started my research career at the same time as the beginning of her life. All through the years, she has given me indescribable delight and enabled me to keep my emotions and daily schedules balanced. I gratefully dedicate this book to my beloved husband and daughter.

Chapter 1

Introduction

Complaining occurs daily in social life. When a participant complains, a sociocultural norm is introduced and interlocutors negotiate whether or not the complained-about act has violated a norm they agree upon. The process of complaining and responding to it also reveals a great deal about the relationship between participants and what sociocultural expectations are constructed in various settings. Complaining is an action expressing dissatisfaction, and can be targeted toward a recipient ("direct complaints," e.g., Dersely and Wooton 2000) or non-present someone or something ("indirect complaints," e.g., Boxer 1993a, 1993b). The act of expressing discontent toward oneself is also a complaint. Complaining can occur in intimate social settings among friends and family members, or it can occur in business settings involving customers, clients, or colleagues. Complaints sometimes involve trivial matters such as misspelling a word, and other times they target serious matters such as causing a car accident. Some complaints are carried out in a jocular way while some cases involve a formal accusation or charge. In order to comprehensively understand complaints, the complainant's action cannot be the sole focus of investigation. Complaining is "ultimately a joint activity, negotiated in a step-by-step fashion between participants in interaction" (Heinemann and Traverso 2009, 2382), and therefore the ways in which a recipient responds to a complaint and how the two parties subsequently manage the interaction about the complainable event are also important parts of a whole complaining activity. This book explores how and why a complaining activity is conducted, particularly by Korean speakers.

In complaining, discontent is expressed because the target behavior fails to meet the complainant's expectations, or he or she considers it to have violated sociocultural norms. Drew (1998) notes that the conduct is not intrinsically or automatically to be regarded as a violation, a transgression, or as reprehensible. It means that the moral reprehensibility of conduct is constituted through the social participant's practices of reporting, describing, and reasoning, with the possibility that there are alternative competing versions of the same conduct. Therefore, certain conduct, which is complained about, is not inherently complainable, but constructed as such through reasoning practices. The reasoning practices are based on selective descriptions and designed for the specific purpose of complaining in the particular context. Such construction of a certain action or event as complainable is then the first step at which the complainant casts his or her perception of complainability into the public domain in order to convince the addressee of the potential transgression. In other words, complainability is to be negotiated, and constructing complainabilty is the first step in the negotiation process. The complaining activity is thus an actual site of social organization in which sociocultural norms are dynamically embodied in concrete shapes.

The dynamic process of constructing complainability and responding to it with acceptance or contention is related to the reason to participate in the complaining activity. While performing complaining and responding to it, the participants embody various social identities and make them specifically relevant to the actions that they are carrying out. The participants' embodiment of their own identities also implies their social relations to others and the memberships that they share. In a complaining activity, a sociocultural norm is brought up, and the participants negotiate whether or not they are operating according to the norm in the social group. The complainant and the recipient(s) therefore partake in the complaining activity as an actual site of social organization in which they can achieve the status of a proper member.

This book explores this dynamic area of human conduct, by investigating (a) systematic patterns of formulating complainability; (b) lexical, grammatical, and prosodic resources for complaints; (c) organizational features of complaining discourse; and (d) the ways in which the participants jointly constitute social identities and cultural norms through complaining. To delve into the complaining activity in Korean, this book analyzes real language use in various contexts such as everyday face-to-face and phone conversation among family members and friends as well as postings on social media platforms, customer reviews online, postings on web communities, news articles, and formal complaints posted on websites of local governments in Korea.

By explicating the aforementioned issues, this book attempts to contribute to our understanding of the relationship between language, interaction, and social organization, particularly in Korean culture. First, as it is inspired by the line of interactional linguistic research, it expands on interpretations of the interplay between grammar and social interaction. In the interactional linguistic approach, researchers have shown how grammar and interaction interrelate in building up each other's concrete form through talk, based on a position that speech is an ongoing or emergent product in a social event and grammar provides one set of resources for accomplishing goals and tasks within the event (e.g., Ochs et al. 1996; Selting and Couper-Kuhlen 2001, among others). Likewise, linguistic formulations are an integral part of constructing complainability in concrete shapes and carrying out the complaining action. The analysis of patterns of doing complaining in Korean will uncover some aspects of the deeply intertwined relationship between the organization of grammar and the organization of social interactional practices.

Second, this volume adds to the body of research that investigates the relationship between language use in talk-in-interaction and social organization. Many sociologists and anthropologists are inspired by Garfinkel's ethnomethodological perspective that social life is a continuous display of member's local understandings of what is going on (Garfinkle 1967). Some have conducted research, using the methodology of Conversation Analysis (henceforth CA), on how social norms and moral dimensions are formulated and accounted for in the actual exchange of talk (e.g., Drew 1998; Pomerantz 1986), and how social identities are negotiated and achieved through the interactional talk of everyday life (e.g., Antaki and Widdicombe 2008; Schegloff 2005). Following this line of research, the current book reveals some of the ways in which social organization, including sociocultural normative standards and identities, is interactively negotiated and constituted through complaining in social interaction.

This study also provides an alternative tool for analyzing the action of complaining in Korean discourse. Much of the research on how Korean speakers complain in Korean or in English has been conducted within the framework of speech act theory (Moon 1996; Murphy and Neu 1996; J. S. Lee 1999), and the prior research has focused on the surface structures of complaining in simplified artificial contexts. By examining real language use in a variety of contexts, this book aims to help us understand how Koreans do complaining and how their complaining action relates to social organization. The analysis of complaining in natural settings will also contribute to second or foreign language learning by way of assisting Korean learners in understanding and developing authentic and effective means of communicating. Korean learners can also develop cultural understanding of normative expectations in Korean society through actual complaining cases presented in this book.

Complaining behavior has been studied in multiple disciplines including CA (e.g., Pomerantz 1986; Drew 1998; Heinemann and Traverso 2009; Schegloff 2005), pragmatics (e.g., Boxer 1993a), cultural communication (e.g., Sotirova 2018), social psychology (e.g., Kowalski 2003), second language acquisition (e.g., Boxer 1993b), and business management (e.g., Balaji et al. 2015). The majority of the previous studies have been on English and other European languages, and therefore this volume contributes to filling the gap by examining complaining in Korean.

1.1. DATA AND METHODOLOGY

With the aim of explicating how Koreans carry out the complaining activity in actual settings, this book uses naturally occurring data only. The data consist of both oral and written discourse in a variety of contexts. The oral data consist of approximately forty telephone conversations and eleven face-to-face conversations. The length of each talk ranges from three minutes to seventy minutes, totaling approximately forty hours. The participants are native speakers of Korean from their teens to their seventies, and the number of people involved is approximately 100. The participants come from all the different provinces in South Korea, but most of them use standard Korean in the recorded data. The participants in the phone conversations and the face-to-face conversations are family members, friends, or neighbors, and therefore they use intimate, non-polite speech styles (*-a/e* or *-(nu)nta*) or informal polite speech style (*-ayo/eyo*) most of the time.

The written data consist of approximately seventy complaints found in customer reviews online, seventy complaints found in postings on Instagram and Twitter, twenty news articles containing complaints, fifty complaints found in postings on two web communities (www.todayhumor.co.kr and www.missyusa.com), and seventy formal complaints posted on the websites of three local governments in Korea (Incheon Metropolitan City, Seoul Metropolitan Council, and Jeju Special Self-Governing Province). The spectrum of formality and speech styles in the written data is wider than that of the oral data. Most of the postings on the social media platforms and some of the customer reviews and the web community postings are highly colloquial, non-polite, and sometimes pseudo-swearing. On the other hand, the news articles and the postings on the local governments' websites show a high level of formality in their texts. The complaints on the local governments' websites are not involved in legal formalities, but they are formal complaints since they demand the governments' proper responses. These complaints employ formal polite speech style (*-(su)pnita*) consistently. In sum, the data corpus of this book covers a wide range of formality and speech styles in the Korean language used in various types of settings in which participants of different ages from diverse regional backgrounds talk or write to others in different relationships. The analysis in this book will therefore help to comprehensively understand linguistic, sociocultural, and communication practices for the complaining activity among Koreans.

The conversational data are closely transcribed according to the conventions used commonly in CA (cf. Ochs et al. 1996, 461–465), and Korean utterances are romanized according to the Yale system (Sohn 1999). Features of interaction such as silence, laugh tokens, and inbreaths are preserved in both Korean utterances and English translations. Some Korean words are translated into English in different ways in different fragments when there is no one-to-one correspondence between the two languages. In such cases, I have tried to choose a translation that seems most suitable for conveying what is going on interactionally.

The methodological framework for explicating complaints, especially in conversations, in this book is CA. CA is an approach to the study of social interaction which takes a perspective that the study of everyday conversation is a primordial locus of social order (Sacks et al. 1974). It has aimed to uncover and describe the organizational features underlying social interaction. CA researchers do not determine categories of analysis beforehand. Instead, they rely on unmotivated observation for locating specific phenomena to analyze. They work with collections of specific practices and closely analyze the participants' moment-by-moment indexing of what is relevant for the participants and how the prior talk is relevant to their subsequent talk. That is, CA research examines the interactants' social displays in talk-in-interaction in a rigorous way, and thereby describes "the procedures by which conversationalists produce their own behavior and understand and deal with the behavior of others" (Heritage and Atkinson 1984, 1).

A significant insight provided by CA research is that social order is "created by participants in talk-in-interaction—jointly, contingently, and always locally" (Ford et al. 2002, 4). Also "[social conduct and social relations] are constituted through our practices of reporting, describing, and reasoning" (Drew 1998, 295), from the CA perspective. CA has thus revealed the importance of explicating the actual exchange of talk that display a central role in constructing social reality and analyzing social order as situated achievements accomplished through coordination among co-participants in particular contexts (see e.g., Antaki and Widdicombe 2008; Drew 1998; Goodwin and Goodwin 1990; Schegloff 2005). The CA perspective is critical to analyzing my data in this book, not only the conversational ones but also the written ones, since the complaining activity is an actual site of social organization in which the participants constitute their social relations and sociocultural norms in the particular contexts.

1.2. OUTLINE OF THE BOOK

Chapter 2 analyzes the types of describing and reasoning practices complainants employ to construct complainability out of a target event. It first demonstrates what specific aspects of target events are recurrently formulated as the grounds for complaining. Then it discusses how complainants further highlight complainable aspects of the target events to intensify the legitimacy of their complaints.

Chapter 3 explicates linguistic resources employed in complaints in Korean. It first explicates linguistic devices that are frequently used to initiate complaints. Then it examines what types of sentences are employed and how those particular sentence types operate to do complaining. It also investigates particular kinds of final intonation often utilized in complaints in oral conversation.

Chapter 4 expands the focus from the characteristics of complaints to a larger structure and examines organizational features of a whole complaining activity from the initial stage to the next responses. It first looks at the initial stage in which participants engage themselves in a projected complaining activity. Then, it investigates how participants respond to a complaint and how they close a complaining activity with or without further expansion. Thereby, it shows how coordinated actions are managed between complainants and recipients throughout the course of the activity.

Chapter 5 presents how particular social identities and memberships are occasioned and moral norms are accounted for while complaining is being performed. The complainants embody various kinds of social identities and make them specifically relevant to the actions that they are carrying out. The complainants' embodiment of their own identities also implies their social relations to others and memberships which they share. By carrying out the complaining action, they point out that the target conduct has violated a certain norm shared among the group members. The complainants and the other participants then negotiate throughout the interaction whether or not they are operating according to the norms in the social group, in order to achieve the status of a proper member. Language use in the specific action therefore operates as a resource for joining the participants together or keeping them apart in particular social ways and that social organization is what the participants negotiate and collaboratively accomplish through their practical actions and reasoning in the local circumstances.

Finally, chapter 6 concludes the book with pedagogical implications and suggestions for further research.

Chapter 2

Formulating Complainability

States of affairs that are complained about are not intrinsically complainable, but are formulated as such through practices of describing and reasoning. Formulating is a means by which speakers construct an explicit sense of a state of affairs by focusing a description of it on some selective aspects of what has happened or is happening. According to Heritage and Watson (1979), formulations can have properties such as "preservation," "deletion," and "transformation" as ways of making particular aspects prominent. In formulating complaints, speakers thus selectively preserve particular aspects of the target conduct with which they are dissatisfied, while deleting the rest, and transform the whole import of the event, for example, from a benign action to a complainable action. One way of using formulations may be to provide accountability of social conduct. Drew (1998, 295) suggests that the accountability of social conduct is constituted through the participants' practices of reporting, describing, and reasoning, and when the participants report their own or others' conduct, their descriptions are themselves accountable phenomena through which they recognizably display an action's (im)propriety, (in)correctness, (un)suitability, (in)appropriateness, (in)justice, (dis)honesty, and so forth. He also maintains that "insofar as descriptions are unavoidably incomplete and selective, they are designed for specific and local interactional purposes." Thus, a certain conduct or event which a speaker complains about is constituted as complainable through the speaker's practices of describing, accounting, and reasoning, and the practices are designed for the specific purpose of complaining in the particular context. Such a formulation of a certain action or event as complainable is therefore the first step at which the speaker casts his or her personal perception into the public domain to convince the addressee of complainability, that is, the first step in the negotiation process.

This chapter explicates how exactly the complainant negotiates complainability with the addressee in social interaction. Schegloff (2005) presents English speakers' practices of recognizing possible complainability before an actual complaint is ever articulated. The analysis in this chapter focuses on more explicit practices of constructing complainability in actual complaints in Korean. It analyzes what kinds of describing and reasoning practices the complainant employs to construct complainability out of the target behavior or state of affairs, and thereupon how he or she negotiates with the addressee regarding why the target event is complainable. It first demonstrates what types of aspects of the target event are recurrently formulated as the grounds for the complaints. Then, it discusses how the complainants further highlight complainable aspects of the target event to intensify the legitimacy of their complaints.

2.1. RECURRENT PATTERNS OF COMPLAINABILITY FORMULATION

Since complaining is an action of expressing dissatisfaction, it involves portraying the target event as negative and troublesome. Then, what sort of negative aspects are typically accentuated in depicting the troublesome event in complaining? I have found four recurrent patterns in my data: (1) to characterize the absence of an expected event as problematic, (2) to acknowledge an expected event but claim it as insufficient, (3) to depict a target event as excessive, and (4) to portray a target event as something unwanted which should not have occurred.

The commonality among the four patterns of formulating complainability is that the complainants articulate a particular feature of the event as a failure to meet a certain expectation or a normative standard in the particular situation. The action of complaining, therefore, reveals the process in which social norms are established and negotiated through the participants' language use in interaction. The following sections illustrate the recurrent patterns of the complainants' practices of describing and reasoning in characterizing a target event as complainable, and then discuss how complaints help negotiate and establish social norms.

2.1.1. Formulating Absence of Expected Event as Complainable

The first pattern of complainability formulation is to construct absence of a certain expected event as complainable. This practice is first noted through an English example by Schegloff (1988). He analyzes that an utterance,

"You didn't get an ice cream sandwich," directed to a roommate who brought other edibles does complaining based on the fact that the speaker's noticing is focused on the absence of the ice cream sandwich, not on what the roommate has actually brought. Using a term, a "negative event," for something which did not happen, he argues that the noticing of the negative event articulates the failure to meet an expectation in the particular context. As he says that complaining regularly involves a practice of noticing of a negative event, the practice of formulating absence of an expected event is frequently utilized as the basis of complainablity in Korean as well.

While it is done through the declarative sentence type in Schegloff's example, the pattern of absence-based formulation for complaining is realized through the interrogative or the imperative format as well as the declarative type in my Korean data. The following social media posting shows an example of the interrogative format.

(1) [Twitter Post, www.twitter.com]

왜 우리 학교에는 바둑 강의가 없는 거야 교양으로 있어야 하는데 왜 없어!

way wuli hakkyo-ey-nun patuk kanguy-ka eps-nun-ke-ya kyoyang-ulo iss-eya ha-nuntey way eps-e!

"Why does our school not have a class on Go? It should have ((one)) for general education, but why doesn't ((it))!"

The complainant who seems to be a lover of the game of Go complains in this posting about his or her school not offering a course on the game. This complaint is delivered through two interrogative sentences, and they formulate absence-based complainability more strongly than Schegloff's example of noticing absence. The complainant not only does notice the absence of the course offering but also does an explicit challenge against it. He or she first implies, in the first sentence, his or her expectation that the school should offer a Go class, and then overtly expresses the expectation in the subordinate clause of the second sentence ("It should have ((one)) for general education, but"). In the context where the expectation is strongly established like this, the two seeming questions with *way* ("why") do not function as real questions asking about the reason for the absence, but as criticizing statements against the absence. The absence of the expected event thus provides the basis for the complainability in this case. (See 3.2.2 for further discussions on how interrogatives with question words do challenging and complaining.)

The following restaurant review posted on a web-based application shows another example of absence-based complainability.

(2) [Restaurant Review 1, www.bdtong.co.kr]

전화를 받아야 주문을 하지 않을까요?

cenhwa-lul pat-aya cwumwun-ul ha-ci anh-ulkka-yo?

"Isn't it that ((I/we)) can place an order only if ((you)) answer the call?"

This review is posted with only one star, which already indicates the reviewer' dissatisfaction with the service of the restaurant. Along with the one-star rating, the complaint is formulated through an interrogative sentence which actually conveys an assertion that a customer can place an order only if the restaurant answers the call. It points to the fact that the expected service of the restaurant answering the call is not available and therefore the reviewer himself or herself cannot place an order. The unavailability of the basic service is a type of absence, which provides the basis of this online complaint.

The practice of absence-based formulation of complainability is observed in oral conversation as well. The following fragment, which is taken from a dinner talk among five close friends, illustrates two complaint utterances. The participants just started to eat in the immediately preceding context and they are eating without talking for a long time (10.5 seconds in line 1 and 7.5 seconds in line 3) at the beginning of this fragment. As background information related to this context, Young is a liaison between the conversation participants and the researcher who asked her to video-record the dinner gathering, and she has asked the other participants not to be conscious of the camera several times in the preceding discourse. In this fragment, she interprets the participants' long non-talking as unusual behavior related to the video-recording, and complains about it in lines 4, 6, and 7.

(3) [Dinner Talk among Five Friends]

```
1      (10.5)
2      Young:  °음°
               °um°
               "°Uhm°"
3      (7.5)
4  →   Young:  *말 좀 해:*        ((l [ a u g h)) ]
               *MAL COM HAY:*    ((l [ a u g h)) ]      * *: ((laugh voice))
               "PLEASE TA:LK ((laugh))"
5      Jeong:                    [((chuckle)) *먹]는 중[에 뭐]*
                                 [((chuckle)) *m]ek-nuncwu[ng-ey mwe]*
                                             * *: ((smile voice))
                                 "((chuckle)) What, ((we)) are in the middle
                                  of eating"
```

6 →	Young:	[왜 일]부러
		[*WAY i*]*lpwule*
7 →		말들을 안 하구 그래:. ((laugh)) .h
		mal-tul-ul an ha-kwu kulay:. ((laugh)) .h

"WHY are ((you guys)) intentionally not saying anythi:ng? ((laugh)) .h"

Young's loud imperative utterance in line 4 brings everybody's attention to the silence, characterizes it as the lack of the expected behavior of having conversation while having a social gathering, and formulates it as a complainable event. The loudness of the utterance is an additional resource for displaying her dissatisfaction. The silence is thus treated as a deliberate and complainable action through Young's loud utterance.

In lines 6 and 7, Young again formulates complainability from the same silence. It is done in the format of negative interrogative with question word *way* ("why"). This seeming question performs complaining by conveying a reversed polarity assertion, "you should've said something ((instead of intentionally staying quiet))!" The complaint is upgraded in this utterance through characterizing the absence of talk as an "intentional (*ilpwule*)" act. In sum, the two complaint utterances shape the silence, which could have been simply a neutral phenomenon, into the participants' unusual conduct of not talking on purpose because of the camera. The absence of talk is hence claimed to be a complainable action, through Young's particular language use for the specific purpose in the particular situation.

2.1.2. Formulating Target Event as Insufficient

The second pattern of formulating complainability is to construct an event as insufficient and claim the insufficiency as complainable. This pattern of formulation is different from the absence-based formulation in that the complainant acknowledges the occurrence of an expected event. However, the complainant claims complainability because he or she considers the event to be still below an expected standard in the particular setting.

The following fragment shows an instance. It is a conversation among three family members, a wife, her husband, and his younger sister who are having a spaghetti lunch.

(4) [Family Lunch] (Slightly Simplified)

1		{(1.0)/((Hus starts eating spaghetti))}
2 →	Hus:	°아유° .h 덜 익었잖아. (이거).
		°*aywu*° .h *tel ik-ess-canh-a. (i -ke).*
		"°*Aywu*° ((they)) are undercooked, you know. (These noodles)."

3   Wife: ↑괜찮은데ː,↑

   ↑*kwaynchanh-unteyː,*↑
   "↑((They)) are OK ((to me)), thoːugh↑"

The husband's utterance produced immediately after having a taste is a response to the state of the spaghetti noodles cooked by the wife. Through various resources, he characterizes the condition of the noodles as too deficient to restrain himself from releasing his negative reaction. In such a characterization, the exclamatory token *aywu* in line 2 plays an important role. It is a response cry which is not completely lexicalized and has no grammatical connection to the other elements of the sentence, but performs an action of expressing the speaker's emotional state (Goffman 1981; Goodwin 1996). A response cry has "the power to elicit the strong reaction visible in the cry" (Goodwin 1996, 394), and thus *aywu* in this fragment enables the husband to characterize and formulate the condition of spaghetti as a matter that has such a powerful force as to elicit his strong reaction. (See 3.1 for further discussions on response cries.)

The situation that has elicited his strong reaction is explicated in the subsequent part of his utterance, *tel ik-ess-canh-a. (i-ke).* ("((They)) are undercooked, you know! (These noodles)."). In this main part of the complaint, he uses the adverb *tel* whose English translation is "less," and claims that the spaghetti noodles are "under"-cooked. With this expression, he formulates his wife's performance as cooking the spaghetti noodles "less than necessary."

The condition of the spaghetti noodles is, however, not below the cooking norm in the absolute sense. The noodles are cooked in a certain state, and the husband claims it to be undercooked according to his own standard through his complaint utterance. However, in line 3, the complainee denies the claim of the undercooked state and presents a different standard of cooking spaghetti. In this line, she utilizes an *-untey*-clause, which is often used in a disaffiliative contexts such as disagreements (Park 1999), and declares that the condition is satisfactory to her. Therefore, the complainability of the target event in this particular context is achieved through the husband's formulation based on his cooking standard, but contested through the wife's response based on her different standard. (See 4.2.4 for discussions on further development of this complaining activity.)

The following excerpt demonstrates another example of complainability formulated by asserting insufficiency. This is an exchange between a wife and a husband who are hosting a pizza gathering for their three close friends. They are preparing fruit for the guests in the following segment.

(5) [Pizza Gathering]

1 {(1.5)/ ((Yun, the wife, sees Suh, her husband, put some peeled fruit onto a plate.))}

2 → Yun: 에게: 더 깎어:

   eykey: te kkakk-e:
   "Eykey: **peel mo:re!"**

3   Suh: 더 깎을 거야:

   te kkakk-ul ke-ya:
   "((I)) WILL peel mo:re!"

Suh, the husband, has peeled a certain amount of fruit and put it on a plate in line 1, and Yun, the wife, displays her noticing of the amount of the fruit in line 2. Her noticing begins with a response cry *eykey:*, which, like *aywu* in Fragment (4), is not a fully lexicalized linguistic item. Whereas most other response cries have no semantic or grammatical features on their own, *eykey* (simplified from the original form, *eykyey* or *aykyay*) conveys the implication that the speaker considers the amount of the target object to be insufficient. The use of this response cry thus enables the speaker to form her noticing as that of an insufficient event. The subsequent utterance also articulates her insufficiency formulation regarding the fruit amount: The command *te kkakk-e:* ("peel more!") presupposes her acknowledgment of Suh's having peeled a certain amount fruit but still claims the necessity of peeling more; in other words, it claims the insufficiency of Suh's behavior. However, the fruit amount is not, again, insufficient in the definite sense. The deficiency is constituted only through the practices that the complainant employs in her utterances. That is, it is simply a particular amount of fruit that has been put onto the plate, but it is observed and characterized as insufficient through Yun's complaint. In this case, the deficiency formulated by Yun is agreed with by the complainee Suh, who claims that he was going to peel more and thus that Yun did not have to tell him.

The practice of insufficiency-based formulation of complainability is found in written discourse as well, and the following data show such examples in customers' reviews online.

(6) [Space Heater Review, www.coupan.com]

완전 가까이에서만 따뜻

wancen kakkai-eyse-man ttattus

"Warm **only when ((I)) am completely close**"

(7) [Hotel Review 1, maps.google.com]

4성급 호텔이라면서 들어가면 **방이 너무 좁고** 화장실 입구는 **싸구려 고리 달린 커텐으로 분리**. 화장실 안도 **매우 좁다**. 슬리퍼도 없고 **물컵은 플라스틱 컵**이 놓여 있다. 라지에타는 요란한 소리를 내서 잠을 잘 수 없었다. 4성급 호텔이 **여관만 못하고** 로비만...

*4 seng-kup hotheyl-i-la-myense tuleka-myen **pang-i nemwu cop-ko** hwacang-sil ipkwu-nun **ssakwulye koli talli-n khetheyn-ulo pwunli**. hwacangsil an-to maywu cop-ta. sulliphe-to eps-ko **mwul-khep-un phullasthik khep**-i nohye-iss-ta. lacieytha-nun yolanha-n soli-lul nay-se cam-ul ca-l swu eps-ess-ta. **4 seng-kup hotheyl-i yekwan-man mos-ha-ko** lopi-man . . .*

"((They)) call it a 4-star hotel but when ((we)) go in, **the room is too small** and the bathroom is **separated with a cheap curtain**. The bathroom space is **very small**, too. There are not even slippers and **the water cups are plastic ones**. The heater makes such loud noises that ((we)) couldn't sleep. **This 4-star hotel is not as good as a motel**, and only their lobby is . . . ."

Given that it is a review on a space heater, the expectation of the consumer in Fragment (6) must have been to get warmed up by using the product. The consumer, however, states that it feels warm "only when he or she is completely close to it (*wancen kakkai-eyse-man*)," which describes its functionality as extremely limited. This review therefore treats the insufficient level of functionality as complainable. In Fragment (7), the customer explicitly indicates a high expectation he or she had for the hotel at the beginning of the review by mentioning "they call it a '4-star hotel'." Then, the reviewer provides the details of how the hotel amenities do not meet his or her expectation, including the small sizes of the room and the bathroom, the bathroom separated only by a cheap curtain instead of a door, and the cheap material for the water cups. All in all, the hotel provides amenities, but they are not at the sufficient level for a four-star hotel, and the low level of the amenities becomes the ground for the complainability in this context.

2.1.3. Formulating Target Event as Excessive

Another way of formulating a triggering event as complainable is to portray it as an "excessive" event. That is, the speakers complain about the target event because they consider it to excessively go beyond a certain normative standard in the particular context. The complainants thus constitute certain aspects of the target event as excessive and thereupon complainable. As an example, Fragment (8) presents a complaint posted on a web community which formulates a child's behavior as problematic based on excessiveness in the noise level.

(8) [Web Community Post 1, www.todayhumor.co.kr]

아이구 아무리 귀엽다구 해도 식당에서 **너무 시끄러운거 아니냐**. 다른 사람도 생각 좀 하지... 참...

*aikwu amwuli kwiyep-takwu hay-to siktang-eyse **nemwu sikkulew-un ke ani-nya**. talun salam-to sayngkak com ha-ci... cham...*

"*Aikwu* no matter how cute ((the kid)) is, **isn't ((he/she)) too loud** in a restaurant? ((The parents)) should think about the other people, too... *Cham*..."

Aikwu at the beginning and *cham* at the end of this fragment are response cries often used in complaint utterances like *aywu* and *eykey:* in Fragments (4) and (5) respectively. The complainer acknowledges the fact that the target of complaining is a child whose behavior can be generally forgivable, but the following remark, "isn't it too loud in a restaurant?," complains that the particular behavior undesirably exceeds the norm and that "they," possibly the parent(s), should be thoughtful toward other people at the restaurant.

The following instance in a product review also presents an explicit yardstick and how the target aspect exceeds an approvable level and therefore is complainable.

(9) [Skin Care Product Review, www.hwahae.co.kr]

용량 대비 **가격이 너무 비싸요**... 토너에 이정도까지 써야 하나 하는 생각

*yonglyang taypi **kakyek-i nemwu pissa-yo**... thone-ey i-cengto-kkaci sse-ya ha-na ha-nun sayngkak.*

"Compared to the amount, **the price is too high**... ((I'm)) wondering if ((I)) had to spend this much ((money)) for toner."

The yardstick for evaluating the skin care product is stated as the amount in the container, and also the fact that the product is toner, which reveals the reviewer's standard that toner should not be expensive. The justification for this complaint is therefore the price of the product at an excessively high level in his or her view.

The practice of complaining based on an excessive aspect is also observed in oral conversation as seen in the following instance. It is a conversation among five close friends at a pizza gathering which is hosted by a married couple, Yun and Suh. Of the conversation participants, Suh, Min, and Won are graduate students in the same department, and Won has mentioned in the previous discourse that he and Min had been on the fourth floor in their departmental building before coming to the gathering. The hostess Yun asks Min in line 1 whether he stayed for a long time on the fourth floor where Won's office is located, and Min answers in line 3 that he went to Won's office because he needed to ask Won a favor regarding his own lab experiment. Without finishing this utterance, Min initiates a complaint toward Won in line 4 that Won showed so much arrogance when Min asked a favor. In lines 6 and 7, Won protests that he did not show any arrogance and produces a counter-complaint that it was Min who brought "all the materials to measure at once."

(10) [Pizza Gathering] (Slightly Simplified)

1 Yun: 사층에 계속 계셨어요?

    sa-chung-ey kyeysok kyeysy-ess-eyo?
    "Did ((you)) stay on the fourth floor for a long time?"

2 (1.0)

3 Min: 아니 뭐 찍는 거 부탁하느라구

    ani mwe ccik-nun ke pwuthakha-nulakwu
    "Well uh because ((I)) needed to ask ((Won)) a favor, some help with measuring"

4   아이구:[: 저 인간 유]세하는 거 때문에 내가 아주,

    aikwu:[: ce inkan ywu]seyha-nun ke ttaymwuney nay-ka acwu,
    "*Aikwu::* because that human being ((/a despicable expression of 'person')) was showing so much arrogance, I was so like"

5 Won: [↑아 유 ː ↑]

    [↑ *a y w u ː ↑*]
    "↑*Aywu::*↑"

6 → Won: >무슨< 유세를 해요: **한꺼번에 저렇게**

    >*mwusun*< *ywusey-lul hay-yo:* **hankkepeney celehkey**

7 →   **다 갖구와가지구:** hu

    ta kackwuw-akacikwu: hu
    "What arrogance did ((I)) sho:w? **((You)) brought all the materials at once like tha:t** hu"

With the expression *hankkepeney celehkey ta kackwuw-akacikwu:* ("You brought all the materials at once like tha:t"), Won calls attention to the amount of the materials which Min brought to him for help and claims that Min needed Won to take care of "all his materials at once (*hankkepeney celehkey ta*)." With this statement, he implies that the amount of work Min brought was too much for him to handle at once and therefore that Min's behavior of bringing an excessive amount of work for help was rather complainable.

Such a formulation of an excessive feature from a certain event as the ground of complainability can be achieved through the use of particular lexical expressions. *Nemwu*, which means "too" is a common lexical resource for it, and it is utilized in Fragment (8) (*nemwu sikkulew-un ke ani-nya.* "isn't it too loud in a restaurant?") and Fragment (9) (*kakyek-i nemwu pissayo* "the price is too high"). Another lexical resource frequently used in Korean is shown in Fragment (11) below. It is an earlier portion of the same conversation as Fragment (10) where five friends are having a social gathering over pizza. Suh in line 1 is the husband of the hosting couple, and Won and Min are guests. Won was working on Lego construction for a long time and the other participants have started eating in the immediately preceding context to the following segment.

(11) [Pizza Gathering]

((Won working on Lego construction, and everybody else gathered at table))

1   Suh: °이따 만들어: 먹구:°

   °*itta mantul-e: mek-kwu:*°
   "°Make it la:ter After eati:ng°"

2   ((several turns deleted: Won keeps working on Lego construction))

3→ Min: 아으 야 자 이 **오바**하지 말구 빨리 피자 먹어::.

   au ya ca i ***opa****-ha-ci mal-kwu ppalli phica mek-e::.*
   "*Au* hey now, don't do ***opa*** ((/'go overboard')), but come and eat the pizza already::."

4   Won: °이게 더 재밌어요:.°

   °*i-key te caymiss-eyo:.*°
   "°This is more fu:n.°"

Since Won keeps working on Lego construction without showing any sign of joining the others at table, Suh in line 1 requests Won to stop and eat first,

18   *Chapter 2*

but Won does not stop building Legos. Min thereupon produces a complaint in line 3, defining Won's conduct as *opa*. The expression *opa* is a colloquial word which originally comes from the English word "over" and refers to an act of doing something to a greater extent than is reasonable. *Opa* in this context refers to Won's act of not joining everybody else in eating and hence delaying the beginning of the gathering as well as playing with the Lego for too long a time. Therefore, such a characterization with the expression *opa*, which is loaded with the speaker's negative affect, formulates Won's act as an excessive behavior and hence plays an important part in making Min's whole utterance do complaining.

2.1.4. Formulating Target Event as Unacceptable

The previous sections have shown examples of complainability formulations with the cases in which complaints are built based on absence, insufficiency, or excessiveness of an expected event. This section, on the other hand, presents cases in which complainability is constructed based on the presence of an unwanted event. The practice in these cases is to characterize a target event as something undesirable which should not have occurred and therefore to claim its presence to be complained about. The following fragment shows an instance. It is taken from a conversation among six teen-aged boys who are playing a card game. While this particular segment of conversation is taking place, one of the participants, Woo, is getting ready to play his card. Min is sitting next to Woo, and he is trying to let the other players know what cards Woo is holding in his hand.

(12) [Card Game]

1   Min: >야 있잖아 뭐냐면< 이야 이.

             >*ya iss-canh-a mwe-nya-myen< i-ya i.*
             ">Hey, you know< ((It)) is two, two."

2   (2.0)

3   Min: *일이야 일. 에이 에이.*

             **il-i-ya il. eyi eyi.*   * *: ((pointing at Woo))
             "((It)) is one, one. A, A. ((/Ace))"

4   (1.2)

5   Hee: *아이 (0.5) 안 되는[데.*

             **ai: (0.5) an toy-nunt[ey.*
             * *: ((looking at his cards in hand))
             "*Ai:* (0.5) but then ((it)) doesn't work ((for me))."

6 →Hoon: [아이 °이거° 이것들이 진짜
[ai °i -ke° i-kes-tul-i cincca

7 → 사기들링을 주고 받는 이: (1.0) 나쁜 놈들.

<u>saki</u>tulling-ul cwu-ko pat-nun i: (1.0) **nappun nom-tul.**
"*Ai* °these°, these guys really, **committing <u>fraud</u> together, the:se** (1.0) **bad guys."**

Min reveals to the other players in line 1 that Woo has a card with a number, two, and then continues to say in line 3 that Woo has an ace card as well. Another player Hee expresses his frustration in line 5 that Min's ace will not work for him, and Hoon thereupon issues a complaint against Min and Hee in lines 6 and 7 that Min and Hee are "bad guys" because they are fraudulently working together on exposing and using the information about Woo's cards. This complaint characterizes the collaborative action between Min and Hee as a *sakitulling*. *Saki* is a Korean word whose meaning is "fraud," and the speaker Hoon seems to blend this word with *-tulling* from a soccer term, *hayntulling* ("handling"), which means a violation of the rule of not touching the ball with a hand. The new word *sakitulling* maintains the original meaning of "fraud" and is used by the speaker as a term which points out a violation at the game. Fraud is a commonsensically and legally unacceptable act which should not occur, and thus by characterizing Min and Hee's act as fraud, Hoon formulates the target behavior as reprehensible and the actors as *nappun nom-tul* ("bad guys") who committed an unacceptable act.

Fragment (13), which follows, is another example in which the target event is portrayed as unacceptable and its occurrence is thereby claimed as the ground of complaining. It is taken from a conversation among three male roommates, Hoy, Jo, and Suk. In this fragment, Hoy is cooking stew for their dinner. In the previous context, he tasted the stew using a spoon to check if the flavor was all right. In line 1, Jo comes to kitchen and grabs the spoon which Hoy used, and Hoy warns him not to use it in line 2, with vocative interjections. Jo, however, continues to use it in tasting the stew in line 3.

(13) [Roommate Talk]

1 {((Hoy is cooking stew in kitchen))

((Jo comes to kitchen and grabs the spoon that Hoy used to taste stew))}

2 Hoy: 야: 야: 야:.
ya: ya:ya:.
"He:y he:y he:y."

3 {(2.2)/((Jo tastes stew and looks at Hoy))}

4 →Hoy: °에이: **추잡스러**°
             *°eyi: **chwucapsule**°*
             "°*Eyi:* **((it)) is disgusting**°"

In response to Jo's act of using the same spoon that he used, Hoy produces a complaint in line 4 which defines Jo's conduct as "disgusting." Through the practice of describing the target behavior as *chwucapsule* ("disgusting"), Hoy defines it as undesirable act which should not have been done. Moreover, Hoy's prior action of warning Jo not to do it in line 2 also shows Hoy's perception of Jo's act as an unwanted one. Thus, by employing the vocative interjections and the particular adjective, Hoy portrays Jo's conduct as unacceptable and builds the complainability on the ground of its unacceptability.

The same way of characterization is found in online postings as well. In the following review on a hotel, the reviewer defines it as the worst at the beginning, and then presents a ground by pointing out the noise from upstairs which should have been prevented if it was a good hotel. This undesirable feature is the basis for the complaint, along with the following remark based on another negative aspect, the insufficient level of drainage in the bathroom.

(14) [Hotel Review 2, www.tripcoupang.com]

최악~~ 윗층 층간 소음 화장실 배수도 잘 안되고

choiak~~ wis-chung chung-kan soum *hwacangsil payswu-to cal an toy-ko*

"**The worst~~. Noise from upstairs.** Bathroom water not draining well, either."

Fragment (15) is a complaint about a neighbor. The complainant characterizes the target person and/or behavior as *cinsang* (a colloquial word meaning "a person or conduct that is too inappropriate to bear to see") from the beginning and then specifies the reason: the act of blowing snow onto the neighbors' yards. It is defined as "crazy/insane" (*michin*) behavior, which displays the complainant's perspective that it is a reprehensible act which should not have been done.

(15) [Web Community Post 2, www.missyusa.com]

옆집 이런 **진상**은 또 처음... 눈 치우는 기계로 **눈을 옆집 마당으로 날리는 미친 이웃** 옆집 때문에 이사가야겠어요!

*yeph-cip ilen **cinsang**-un tto cheum. . . nwun chiwu-nun kikyey-lo **nwun-ul yeph-cip matang-ulo nalli-nun michi-n iwus** yeph-cip ttaymwuney isaka-ya-keyss-eyo!*

"My neighbor, ((I)) have never seen a **moron** like this. . . . **This crazy neighbor who blows the snow to the next houses** with a snow blower. ((I)) will have to move because of this neighbor!"

2.1.5. Summary

This chapter has thus far shown that complaints are formulated based on absence, insufficiency, or excessiveness of an expected event, or presence of an unwanted event in Korean. Each section has focused on one type of complainability formulation, but the four types are often employed with mixture within a complaint. As pointed out in the previous section, Fragment (14) is an example in which a complaint about a hotel is constructed based on a combination of an unacceptably present feature ("the worst noise level from upstairs") and an insufficient aspect ("the insufficient level of drainage in the bathroom").

Absence, deficiency, excessiveness, or unacceptability of the target event is embodied through the speakers' selective descriptions, and its complainability or reprehensibility is constituted via the complainants' reasoning practices of the wrongness of the target event. The practices of building absence, insufficiency, excess, or unacceptable presence of the target event as the basis for complaining point to a normative standard for a particular context. For example, in Fragment (5), in which the wife complains toward her husband based on her observation that the amount of fruit is insufficient for the guests, she proposes a social norm of providing a certain amount of food to the guests at a social gathering, and the husband co-participates in constructing it as a social standard by displaying the same orientation. In Fragment (10) as well, the participants exhibit an expectation that one is not supposed to show arrogance to his friend who asks for help, and that one is not supposed to ask for too much help from his friend, and thereby collaboratively construct these as social standards. The normative standards implied through complaint utterances therefore provide the complainants with important resources for formulating the target behavior in a particular way and expanding the scope of their personal dissatisfaction regarding the behavior to a socially shared extent.

The proposed normative standards are not, however, accepted by the complainees in every case. For instance, in Fragment (4), in which the husband complains to his wife about the state of the spaghetti noodles, he claims the noodles to be undercooked according to his interpretation of the cooking norm. Since the physical state of the noodles is the same for the husband and the wife, it is their different concepts of the cooking standard that differentiate their evaluative positions. The negotiation strategy of proposing a certain expectation as a normative standard for the context in order to thereupon convince the addressees of the complainability of the target behavior, then, is not always

22   *Chapter 2*

successful. The action of complaining, therefore, reveals the negotiation process in which the participants dynamically form a variety of normative standards into certain concrete shapes by proposing, contesting, or affirming them.

2.2. INTENSIFYING FORMULATION

This section discusses further practices employed by complainants to legitimize their claim of the complainability of the target event. Through analysis of the complaint talk, Korean speakers are found to often use intensifying expressions to emphasize their formulations of absence, insufficiency, or excessiveness of the target behavior in building their complaint utterances and thereby to strengthen their claim of complainability. In complaints about an unacceptably present event, they characterize its occurrence as repetitive and propose that the target behavior is not an incident which has accidentally happened but an unacceptable action which the complainee has repeatedly committed and is thus responsible for.

Complaining is the first step in the negotiation process to convince the recipients of complainability of the target event. However, complainability first formulated by the complainant is not always accepted by the complainee, as demonstrated in a preceding section through the fragments where two participants disagree in terms of showing arrogance to a friend who needs help and asking for too much help from a friend. Employing intensifying expressions is thus a strategy that complainants use to maximize legitimacy and attempt to avoid anticipated denials by the complainees or disagreements by third parties. English speakers are also found to frequently use "extreme case formulations" to assert the strongest case in anticipation of non-sympathetic hearings in complaining (Pomerantz 1986).

2.2.1. Emphasis on Absence of Expected Event

Let me first illustrate how a complainant highlights the lack of an expected event, when formulating its absence, with the use of a variety of linguistic expressions in Korean. Fragment (16) contains an example.

(16) [Restaurant Review 2, www.bdtong.co.kr]

도대체 언제 갖다 주시나요? **한 시간이 넘**었는데. 전화 **수십 통을 해도** 안 받으시네요.

totaychey ence kacta cwu-si-na-yo? **han sikan-i nem**-*ess-nuntey. cenhwa* **swusip thong-ul hay-to an** *pat-usi-ney-yo.*

Formulating Complainability 23

"When in the world are you going to bring ((the food))? It has been **over an hour.** ((You)) don't answer the phone **even though ((I)) call dozens of times.**"

In this review on a restaurant, the reviewer produces a complaint in the first sentence based on the absence of the expected food delivery. The reviewer continues complaining in the following parts based on an excessive amount of waiting time and the lack of a basic service of answering customers' calls. The complainant emphasizes the reprehensibility of the target event by specifying the duration of waiting time and the number of calls he or she has made. Specifying the long waiting time ("over an hour") and the number of unanswered calls ("dozens of times") is a strategy to appeal to the audience in a more convincing way.

We can see another instance in Fragment (17), in which two high school girls are talking over the phone, the caller Nami complains in lines 4 and 5 that Eun never calls her if she does not call Eun.

(17) [Phone Conversation between Two High School Girls]

((Nami is calling her friend Eun.))

1   Eun: 여보세요:?

           yeposeyyo:?
           "Hello:?"

2   Nami: 나 나미다.

           na Nami-ta.
           "This is Nami."

3   Eun: 응: 오랜만이네?

           u:ng. olayn-man-i-ney?
           "Yea:h. Long time no see!"

4 →Nami: 어찌 **내가 전화 안 하면** 전화

           *ecci **nay-ka cenhwa-l an ha-myen** CENHWA-L*

5 →   **한 통화도** 안 하냐?

           HAN THONGHWA-TO an ha-nya?
           "How come ((you)) **NEVER MAKE A SINGLE PHONE CALL** ((to me)) **if I don't call ((you))**?"

After Eun opens the phone conversation with "hello" in line 1, Nami self-identifies in line 2. Eun acknowledges Nami's self-identification and then greets in line 3. Then, Nami produces a complaint in the format of a question with *ecci* ("how" or "why") in lines 4 and 5. This seeming question conveys an assertion "you never make a single phone call to me if I don't call you," and thereby formulates Eun's lack of effort to keep up their phone communication as complainable. This utterance is designed to further emphasize Eun's lack of effort in order to strengthen the complainability. First, this negative question type of utterance employs intensifying expressions, *HAN THONGHWA-TO an* ("not even a single phone call"). The utterance can convey the same meaning and do the same action without the phrase, *HAN THONGHWA-TO*, but the addition of this phrase much more highlights the absence of Eun's desirable effort between close friends. Moreover, the intensifying expressions are produced with louder voice and the word *HAN* ("one/single") among those expressions is stressed, which farther underscores the absence of the expected act as complainable.

There is another way that this utterance is designed to strengthen the complainability of the target event: Using the subordinate clause, *nay-ka cenhwa-l an ha-myen* ("if I don't call you"), Nami strongly contrasts the absence of Eun's endeavor with her own effort, which brings up a social norm that there should be a mutual effort between friends to maintain communication. Nami's utterance thus articulates the unbalanced effort between herself and Eun, and thereby formulates the target event as Eun's unacceptable behavior as a friend. Such a formulation of the target event as an accusable one in contrast with her own efforts, along with the definite negative characterization of Eun's lack of effort, makes such a strong case of complainability that it leaves little room for Eun to provide justifiable grounds for not having made a phone call.

The following is another absence-based complaint utterance which highlights the negative aspect. It is taken from a phone conversation which Eun is having with another friend Jeon. Eun, Jeon, and some other school friends are members of a web community, and all of them except Eun are gathered at Jeon's place for a party. So Jeon calls Eun and complains in the following lines that Eun is missing from the party.

(18) [Phone Conversation among High School Girls]

1 →Jeon: 야 오늘 우리 ㄷ-- **다** 모여서 고기 구워먹기로

*ya onul wuli t-- **ta** moy-ese koki kwuwe mek-ki-lo*

2 →   했**는데** 너**만** 안 왔어˸

*hay-ss-**nuntey** ne-**man** an wa-ss-e˸*
"Hey we have decided to gather for a meat party a-- **all together** today, **but** you are the **only** one who hasn't co˸me!"

In building Eun's absence at the gathering as the basis for the complaining action, Jeon emphasizes the contrast between "all" the other members who are present and Eun, who is the only one missing, with the use of the contrastive connective *-nuntey* (Choi 1991) and two linguistic elements *ta* ("all") and *-man* (a particle meaning "only"). Additionally, by saying that it was the community's decision to have the gathering, Jeon formulates Eun's absence as a failure to play a role as a good member of the community, which intensifies the complainability of the target event.

In the later talk in the same conversation as seen in (19), Eun in turn does a complaining action toward Jeon about her friends' failure to notify her:

(19) [Phone Call among High School Girls]

1 → Eun: *이 자식들. .h 나한테 그 연락 **하나**

  I CASIK-TUL. .h NA-HANTHEY KU YENLAK **HANA*

2 → 못 하냐?*

  MOS HA-NYA?*   * *: ((pretending-anger voice))
  "THESE JERKS. .h ((YOU)) COULDN'T EVEN CONTACT ME?"

In this complaint, Eun maintains that they should have contacted her but did not. Her friends' act of not contacting her is therefore reprehensible in her formulation. The word *HANA* ("one") in this utterance is used to increase complainability of the target event. *Hana* is originally a numeral classifier meaning "one," but it has another type of usage with the meaning of "not even (something)" in a negative sentence. The use of *HANA* in this example modifies *yenlak* ("contact") and characterizes it as a very easy thing to do. The whole utterance not only points to a failure to notify her but also formulates the non-action as a failure to do an effortless thing, and hence fortifies the complainability even further.

2.2.2. Emphasis on Insufficiency of Target Event

As discussed earlier, complainants sometimes build a complaint utterance in a way that the target event is characterized as unacceptably insufficient for a certain expectation or normative standard in the given context. The following example shows a complaint in which insufficiency of the complainable action is further underscored through the use of a linguistic resource such as a diminutive form. The following fragment is a conversation between two female roommates who are hosting a dinner gathering with three close friends. The hosts, Young and Jeong, have been cooking a stew as the main dish for the dinner, and Young complains in line 1 about Jeong's prior act of putting a vegetable into the stew.

(20) [Dinner Talk among Five Friends]

((Young comes to the table and looks into the stew pot. Then she grabs a plate with a vegetable and puts some into the stew.))

1 →Young: *더 많이 눃지: 왜 **요**만큼 넜대:*

        te manhi nuh-ci: way **yo-mankhum ne-ss-tay:**
        * *: ((keep putting vegetable into the stew))
        "((You)) should've put mo:re. Why did ((you)) put **this** litt:le?"

2   {(0.5)/ ((Young keeps putting vegetable into the stew.))}

3   Young: 이쁨-- 이쁨[만] 강조했구나.

        ippum-- ippum[-ma]n kangcohay-ss-kwuna.
        * *: ((keep putting vegetable into the stew))
        "Pretti-- ((you)) were just emphasizing the p̲rettiness ((of it)), right."

4   Jeong: [반--]

        [*pan--*]
        "Half--"

5   {(.)/ ((Young keeps putting vegetable into the stew.))}

6   Jeong: 반씩 (.) 이따 (넣을)라구.

        pan-ssik (.) itta (neh-ul)lakwu.
        "Half (.) ((I)) was gonna put the other half later."

In line 1, the particular amount of the vegetable, which Jeong has put into the stew is characterized as insufficient, which is a claim that her performance is a failure to reach a cooking standard. In defining the insufficiency of the amount of vegetable in the stew, Young emphasizes the scantiness by utilizing *yo*, a diminutive form of the proximal demonstrative *i* ("this"), which indicates that the size or the amount of the referent is small. She produces the diminutive demonstrative with stress, and this particular practice increases the emphasis on the scantiness and strengthens the complainability of the target event even further.

The diminutive form is recurrently employed to intensify the degree of complainability constructed based on insufficiency. Fragments (21) and (22) show instances in a social network posting and a news headline.

(21) [Instagram Post, www.instagram.com]

에게 겨우 **요**만큼 주고 그 가격이라니 앞으로 과카몰리는 집에서 걍 해먹는 걸로~~.

*eykey kyewu **yo**-mankhum cwu-ko ku kakyek-i-lani aph-ulo kwakhamolli-nun cip-eyse kyang hay-mek-nun kel-lo~~.*

"*Eykey* serving only **this** little at that price! ((I've decided)) to make guacamole just at home in the future~~."

(22) [News Report 1, www.hani.co.kr]

기대치 저만큼... 추진력은 **요**만큼

자통법 이후 주어진 과제

자본력 수준 미흡... 감독당국 준비 태세도 의문

*kitaychi ce-mankhum... chwucinlyek-un **yo**-mankhum*
cathongpep ihwu cwueci-n kwacey
caponlyek swucwun mihup... kamtok-tangkwuk cwunpi thaysey-to uymwun

"Expectation Level That Much High... Driving Force **This** Little
Given Task After Capital Market Integration
Capital Level Insufficient... Authorities' Preparedness Also Questionable"

Fragment (21) is a complaint about the miniscule amount of food served in a restaurant. The response cry (*eykey*), which implies the amount is too small and the next word, *kyewu* ("only"), already formulate the posted remark as a complaint, and the diminutive *yo* puts more emphasis on the small amount. The news headline and the two following subheadlines in Fragment (22) display the criticizing stance against the authorities who implemented a new policy. The criticism is formulated through many lexical choices targeting the insufficient levels of the driving force for the new policy, the capital, and the preparedness of the authorities. The diminutive form *yo* of the lexical choices heightens the degree of the criticism: *Yo* is typically used in informal contexts, and its unconventional use in the main headline of a news which is a formal text type is to put more stress on the targeted insufficiency.

In addition to the diminutive demonstrative *yo*, the response cry *eykey* is often employed in insufficiency-based complaints to put emphasis, as exemplified in Fragments (5) and (21). Fragment (23) is an additional example in a news headline.

(23) [News Report 2, autotimes.hankyung.com]

"**에게게**! 이게 뭐야" 자동차 번호판 파동 재연

"*eykeykey! i-key mwe-ya*" *catongcha penho-phan phatong cayyen*

"'***Eykeykey***! What is this!' Commotion about Vehicle Registration Plates Recurring"

This news headline consists of two parts: The first part delivers the public's negative exclamation and the second component specifies what the negative exclamation is about. The public's exclamation in the first part is composed of informal language such as a response cry (*eykeykey*, an emphasized variation of *eykey*[1]) and a rhetorical question in an intimate speech style (*i-key mwe-ya*, "What is this!"). Neither of these is conventionally used in formal texts, but the news headline utilizes the informal language with quotation marks to convey the public's "unfiltered" complaining stance toward the issue. *Eykeykey!*, the response cry in this case, is an emphasized variation of *eykey* seen in earlier fragments, and an exclamation mark is added to it. Both of these features fortify the complaining stance displayed through the rhetorical question, "what is this!"

2.2.3. Emphasis on Excessiveness of Target Event

Intensifying expressions are also used in complaints formulated based on excessiveness, making the inordinate aspects more prominent. The following is an online posting in which a mother complains about her daughter's excessive demand.

(24) [Web Community Post 3, www.missyusa.com]

1   딸 키우시는 엄마분들... 이 짓을 언제까지 하나요? ㅠ

   ttal khiwu-si-nun emma-pwun-tul. . . i-cis-ul encey-kkaci ha-na-yo? ㅠ

   "Those of you moms who raise daughters. . . How long should ((I)) do this stupid thing? ㅠ'

2   4살 딸 키우고 있는데 **하루종일** 역할놀이에 **빠져 있**어요.

   4 sal ttal khiwu-ko iss-nuntey **halwu-congil** *yekhal-noli-ey* **ppacy-e iss**-*eyo*.
   "((I)) have a 4-year old daughter and ((I)) am **dragged into** role-play **all day long**."

3   **인형놀이, 캠핑놀이, 공주놀이, 슈퍼놀이, 병원놀이,**

   inhyeng-noli, khaymphing-noli, kongcwu-noli, sywuphe-noli, pyengwen-noli,

   "Doll-play, camping-play, princess-play, market-play, hospital-play,"

4   식당놀이, 엄마놀이, 아기 놀이, 선생님 놀이... 등등등...

   siktang-noli, emma-noli, aki-noli, sensayngnim-noli... tung-tung-tung...

   "restaurant-play, mom-play, baby-play, teacher-play... etc. etc. etc...."

5   네.. 한두번 해주긴 하죠...

   ney.. han-twu-pen hay-cwu-ki-n ha-cyo...

   "Yes... ((I)) do it a couple of times..."

6   하지만 너무 재미없잖아요 ㅠㅠ

   haciman nemwu caymi-eps-canh-ayo ㅠㅠ

   "But ((it)) is no fun at all ㅠㅠ"

7   말도 **반복반복**.. 레파토리도 **반복**...

   *mal-to **panpok-panpok**.. leyphatholi-to **panpok**...*

   "**Repeating and repeating** the same words... **Repeating** the same repertoire, too..."

8   아... 힘들어요 ㅠㅠ

   a... himtul-eyo ㅠㅠ

   "A... ((it)) is hard ㅠㅠ"

9   **도대체** 이거 언제까지 하나요... 하..

   ***totaychey** i-ke encey-kkaci ha-na-yo... ha..*

   "How long **the heck** do ((I)) have to do this... ha.."

10 이정도 키우면 더 쉬워질 줄 알았는데 정말 누워있는

   i-cengto khiwu-myen te swuiw-eci-l-cwul al-ass-nuntey cengmal nwuw-e iss-nun

11 아기 때가 100배는 편하네요 ㅠㅠ 흑..

   aki-ttay-ka 100 pay-nun phyenha-ney-yo ㅠㅠ *huk..*

   "((I)) thought it would get easier at this age, but it was 100 times easier when ((she)) was a baby just lying ㅠㅠ *huk..*"

The complaining stance of the writer of this posting is conveyed in line 1 through the lexical choice of *cis* ("negative behavior") and the emoticon, ㅠ,

which symbolizes an eye shedding tears. The negative behavior, which the writer complains about, is specified in line 2 as a set of role-plays that she is forced to interact in with her four-year-old daughter. The complainant intensifies the complaint by claiming that she is "dragged into" (*ppacy-e iss*) it "all day long" (*halwu-congil*), which indicates the highly excessive level of her daughter's demands. She continues to emphasize the excessive aspect in lines 3 and 4 by specifically laying out all the different types of role-play she has been involved in. She adds "etc." three times after laying out nine different types, which implies that her daughter demands countless types of role-play. More lexical items in lines 7 and 9 such as *panpok-panpok* ("repeating and repeating"), *panpok* ("repeating"), and *totaychey* ("the heck") are also used to highlight the complained-about aspect.

Fragment (25) below shows another example of using an adverb to emphasize the excessive feature of the complainable event. It is taken from a conversation among two mothers of young children and one grandmother. The two participants are a mother (Mom) and a grandmother (Gran) of a three-year-old girl named Mijin, and they are talking about Mijin to a two-year-old boy's mother who has become a friend through play-dates for their two children. They are talking about some difficulties in disciplining the child. In line 1, Grandma mentions Mijin's improper habit at meal time and goes further to complain through line 5 that it takes too long to feed her, do her hair, and dress her because she does not stay still. Upon this complaint toward Mijin by Grandma, Mijin's mother says that there is a cause for her improper eating habit (lines 7 and 8), and specifies the cause as the grown-ups' excessive care of following her around to feed her (lines 8 and 9). In line 9, Mom further specifies "the grown-ups" as "Grandma" and thereby directs the responsibility for the child's improper habit to Grandma and formulates a complaint to her up to line 10.

(25) [Caregiver Talk] (Slightly Simplified)

1   Gran: ↑밥을 앉아서 안 먹어요↑ 지금도:,

   ↑*pap-ul anc-ase an mek-eyo*↑ *cikum-to:,*

   "↑((Mijin)) doesn't sit still while eating↑ even no:w,"

2   °꼭:° 떠 먹여가지고:° °(그렁께)°

   °*kko:k*° *ttey-meyky-ekaciko:* °(*kulengkkey*)°
   "°every ti:me° ((we)) have to spoon up food and fee:d ((her))
   °and so°"

3   <밥 먹는 시간:> 뭐, .h <머리 빗는 시간:>

   <pap mek-nun sika:n> mwe, .h <meli pis-nun sika:n>
   "<the time for ea:ting> and like, .h <the time for doing ((her)) hai:r>"

4   머리도 가마이 안 앉았응께 따라(댕기)면서

   meli-to kamai an anc-ass-ungkkey ttala(tayngki)-myense

5   빗:긴다구 °저 에미(는)° .h 옷도 그러제: (1.5)

   pi:ski-nta-kwu °ce eymi-(nun)° .h os-to kule-cey: (1.5)
   "((her)) ha:ir, too, because ((she)) would not sit still, °her mom° has to follow ((her)) around, you know .h the same with ((her)) clo:thes (1.5)"

6   >아들이 어디 [가(자구)하면<]

   >a-tul-i eti [ka-(cakwu)-ha-myen<]
   ">so if they say ((they)) (should) to go somewhere then<"

7   Mom: [개는 밥을] (0.3) °u° 당연히 안 앉아 먹게 돼

   [kyay-nun pap-ul] (0.3) °u° tangyenhi an anc-a mek-key tway

8   있어: 어른들이 *쫓아다니면서 먹이니까*

   -iss-e: elun-tul-i *ccochatani-myense .h meki-nikka
   * *: ((laugh voice))
   "She has her meal (0.3) °u° it's no wonder she turns out not to sit still for ea:ting because grown-ups follow ((her)) around and spoonfeed her"

9 → 할머니가 **계::속** 쫓아다니면서 먹이는데:, .h

   *halmeni-ka **kyey::sok** ccochatani-myense (mek)i-nuntey:, .h*
   "Grandma follows her around and spoonfeeds ((her)) **a::ll the time**, and so .h"

10 → 걔가 <u>왜</u> *와서 거기* 앉아 있겠어:

   kyay-ka <u>way</u> *wa-se keki* anca iss-keyss-e:
   * *: ((smile voice))
   "<u>why</u> would she come and sit still there, you kno:w"

In lines 9 and 10, Mom complains toward Grandma that Grandma follows Mijin around to spoonfeed her so that she has turned out to have the bad manners of moving around at meal time. Mom characterizes Grandma's care for Mijin as excessive and builds her complaint based on it. She also uses the modal marker *-keyss* (line 10), through which Korean speakers can "provide affective information about a situation being talked about" (Kim and Suh 1993, 102), and displays her dissatisfied "affective stance." Further, she employs the adverb *kyey::sok* ("constantly") to emphasize the excessive feature of the target conduct. The use of this word typifies Grandma's act of following Mijin to spoonfeed her as a constant, regularized one, and hence formulates it not simply as an excessive act but as a persistent one, which is therefore more complainable. The way of pronouncing this adverb with great lengthening also delivers the emphasis of the constant, improper feature of the target behavior.

The two examples presented above demonstrate how expressions with the semantic features of repetitiveness or continuance are used in complaints to highlight the excessive aspects of the target behavior. These expressions are used to underscore that it is the excessiveness of the target behavior that is undesirable. That is, the behavior itself in each example is not formulated as particularly undesirable by the complainants: The complainant in Fragment (24) does not characterize role-pay itself as complainable and Mom in Fragment (25) does not build her complaint based on Grandma's care itself, either. Not these acts, but the excessive aspects of these acts are articulated as the basis for the complaints, and the expressions, *halwu-congil* ("all day long"), *panpok* ("repeating"), and *kyey::sok* ("constantly"), are utilized as resources for intensifying the complaints.

2.2.4. Emphasis on Repetitiveness of Unacceptable Target Event

Expressions with the semantic features of repetitiveness or continuance are also employed in complaints against unacceptable target events which should not have occurred. In this type of complaints, the presence of the target behavior itself is formulated as complainable, and the use of expressions with the meanings, "repeatedly," "constantly," and the like, therefore provides further resources to increase the complainability. We can see an example in Fragment (26) below. It is taken from the conversation among five friends at a pizza gathering. In the immediately prior discourse, Min teased Won by saying that Won has a skilful strategy to take more food in competition with others. Then in line 1 below, Yun, the wife of the hosting couple, says that Won's skill is impressive and that her husband Suh also behaves like that. In lines 3 and 5, she continues to tell the participants how Suh "instinctively" takes the best portions of food at the table, and Suh expresses his disagreement in the middle of Yun's attempt to characterize his eating habit as competing to win delicious food. Suh first reveals his disagreement by repeating

Yun's wording *ponnungcekulwu* ("instinctively") followed by an exclamatory token *cham* ("oh my") in line 4, and then complains in lines 6 and 7 that she acts like that all the time:

(26) [Pizza Gathering] (Slightly Simplified)

1   Yun: 야 하 .h 너 대단하다 우리 신랑이 그렇거든¿

         ya ha .h ne taytanha-ta wuli sinlang-i kuleh-ketun¿

         "Hey ha .h you're impressive. My husband is like that, you know¿"

2   Min: *↑어[:: ↑]

         *↑*E* [*: :* ↑]   *: ((looks at Suh))

         "↑O::h↑"

3   Yun: [본능]적으루 그렇게 돼요:.=

         [*ponnung*]*cekulwu kulehkey tway-yo:.*=

         "Instinctively, ((he)) doe:s it."

4   Suh: =*°본능적으(루) 참°* [h

         =*°*ponnungceku(lwu) cham*°* [h   * *: ((laugh voice))

         "°Instinctively, oh my°"

5   Yun: [>근데 뭐< 먹을 [게 딱]

         [>*kuntey mwe*< *mek-ul* [*key ttak*]

         ">and like< there is this food <u>right</u> here"

6 → Suh: [***맨날**]

         [****maynnal***]

7 →   이런대니까*=

         ile-ntay-nikka*=   * *: ((laugh voice))

         "((She)) acts like this **all the time**, you know"

8   (Won): =((laugh))

In his utterance in lines 6 and 7, *maynnal ile-ntay-nikka* ("She acts like this all the time, you know"), Suh uses a pro-verbal form *ileta* ("do like this") to refer to Yun's prior act, which is speaking negatively of his eating habits in front of other people. By using a pro-verb instead of specifying what kind of act she was exactly doing, Suh characterizes the particular act which Yun is doing at this particular moment as just part of what she usually does. In other words, he forms a complaint toward the particular action that Yun has just done, and also toward the similar pattern of acts that she frequently does. With the use of the connective -*nikka*, which is used sometimes to provide an affective ground for a complaint (Kim and Suh 1994), he also displays his dissatisfied state and invites the other participants' alignment with his trouble. Furthermore, the adverb *maynnal* ("everyday/all the time") further intensifies the constant aspect of the target behavior. Characterizing the target conduct as Yun's constant behavioral pattern prevents the target act from being interpreted as an incident, which has just inadvertently happened. It instead formulates the case as an action which the complainee performs repeatedly of her own will and thus has to take the full responsibility for. That is, through the use of the adverb *maynnal*, he builds the target behavior as a constant, unacceptable act that is attributable to Yun, highlights repetitiveness and regularity, and thereby increases the complainability of the target event.

Another adverb with the meaning of "again," *tto* is utilized as a resource to build and emphasize the repetitiveness of an unacceptable event in the following complaint example. Fragment (27) is a later portion of Fragment (26) above. In the talk following (26), a guest Min asked Suh what Yun was talking about regarding Suh's eating habit, which led to Suh's telling that she was talking about his way of eating a vegetable side-dish, *kimchi*. Suh argued that although it is not true, his wife Yun keeps saying that he skillfully picks only nice pieces from a bowl, which they both share and so relatively bad pieces are left for her. He also said that Yun always scolds him about it, and then in lines 1, 3, and 4 in the following fragment, he continues to say that Yun treats him so harshly because of it that he was almost going to have two separate bowls of *kimchi* on the table. Upon Suh's blaming for her treating him very badly, Yun issues a counter-complaint in line 5:

(27) [Pizza Gathering] (Slightly Simplified)

1   Suh: <u>하</u>:두 구박해가지구 .h 김치를 <u>두</u> 그릇을

<u>ha</u>:twu kwupakhay-kacikwu .h kimchi-lul <u>twu</u> kulus-ul

2   떠 놓고 먹(h)을(h)려(h)구 하(h)다(h)가(h) hu

tte noh-ko mek(h)-ul(h)lye(h)kwu ha(h)-ta(h)ka(h) hu

"Because ((she)) treats me <u>so</u>: harshly that .h" ((I)) was almost going to put <u>two</u> bowls of *kimchi* on table when eat(h)ing(h), but(h) hu"

3 → Yun: ↑아:우:::↑ 진짜 **또** 시작이야

↑*a:wu:::*↑ *cincca **tto** sicak-i-ya*

"↑A:wu:::↑ really, ((you)) are starting ((this)) **again**"

4 내 [가 그랬지 .h]

nay[-ka kulay-ss-ci .h]

"I told you this .h"

5 Won: [어 싸우면 안 돼요]=여기 카메라 찍혀요.=

[*e̱ ssawu-myen an tway-yo]=yeki khameyla ccikhy-eyo.*=

"O̱h, ((you)) cannot fight. It is videotaped here."=

6 Yun: =밖이 오-- 밖이 오면-- 밖이 오면은:, 어? (0.5) 남

=*pakk-i o-- pakk-i o-myen-- pakk-i o-myen-u:n, e? (0.5) nam*

7 들이 오면밖에서는 (1.0) 나를 칭̱찬하는

tul-i o-myen pakk-eyse-nun (1.0) na-lul chi̱ngchanha-nun

8 거를 좀 배워라 했̱었잖아.

ke-lul com payw-ela ha̱y-ss-ess-canh-a.

="Outside--, if ((we)) are outside--, if we're out in public, you know? (0.5) If other people come, at least with other people (1.0), please learn to pra̱ise me, ((I)) told ((you)), didn't ((I))."

In line 3, Yun expresses her dissatisfied emotional state through the high-pitched response cry ↑*a:wu:::*↑ and then issues a complaint that Suh is starting the same thing all over again. Since Suh did a blaming toward Yun in his immediately preceding turn, what Yun refers to can be heard as his action of blaming her. However, she does not specify what kind of thing Suh is starting again, and thereby typifies his act in this particular context as part of what he often does. Similar to the complaint in (26), Yun's complaint in this segment formulates complainablity based on Suh's behavior in the immediate setting but builds up a stronger ground, through the use of a general verb, on its routinized pattern, which turns out in lines 8 through 10 to be criticizing her even in front of other people. Furthermore, the employment of the adverb *tto* ("again") in the complaint in line 5 adds more emphasis on the repetitive and constant aspect in formulating Suh's behavior as a reprehensible action, and thereby strengthens the basis of complaining.

The following segment shows an interesting case of using the adverb *tto* in complaining. This fragment is taken from a conversation among five friends at a dinner gathering hosted by two roommates, Young and Jeong. To provide more background information for better understanding of this fragment, all the participants are single, Young is in her mid-twenties and Joo a female guest in her mid-thirties. Joo and Hoon are sister and brother. In the immediately preceding talk, Young said that their rice cooker does not work very well, and Joo recommended that she buy an electronic pressure rice cooker because it makes great-tasting rice. Young responded that she could not buy one because it is very expensive, and it would not be necessary anyway because she would not have any chance to get married soon. That is, Joo's suggestion of buying a nice rice cooker leads into bringing up Young's sociocultural standard that single women do not need to buy expensive appliances until they have a specific wedding plan. At this point of the talk, Joo issues a complaint in line 1 toward Young.

(28) [Dinner Talk among Five Friends]

1   Joo: 야 결혼 안 하면 맛있는 거 먹으면 안 돼?

             ya kyelhon an ha-myen masiss-nun ke mek-umyen an tway?

             "Hey if not married, can ((we)) not eat delicious food?"

2   Hoon: ((ch[uckle))

3   Young: [((chuckle)) ((l [a u g h))]

4   Hoon: [((chuckle))]

5   Young: [미안해 s::   [((l a u g h))]

             [*mianhay s::*   [((l a u g h))]

             "I am sorry s:: ((laugh))"

6   Joo: [>마-- 맛있는 거 먹어야 [지< ( )]

             [>*ma-- masiss-nun ke mek-eya*[*-ci*< ( )]

             ">Del-- ((we)) have to eat delicious things anyway<"

7 → Hoon: [왜 **또** 결혼] 얘기를 해서 **또**

                                 [*way* **tto** *kyelhon*] *yayki-lul hay-se* **tto**

8 → 우리 누나를 [**또** 건드려 **또:**]

wuli nwuna-lul [***tto** kentuly-e **tto:***]

"Why do you **again** talk **again** about marriage **again** and so irritate my sister **aga:in**?"

9 Young: [((l a u g] h)) .h

With her utterance in line 1, Joo displays another kind of normative orientation that anybody, whether or not married or planning to get married, can buy a nice rice cooker for their own selves. As mentioned earlier, Joo is a single woman who is much older than Young. According to the sociocultural norm that Young has brought up in the preceding context, Joo could be considered to have wasted money on buying an expensive rice cooker even without getting married. Joo's utterance in line 1 thus makes visible this implication of Young's normative orientation and thereby challenges and complains toward Young's act of raising the issue of marriage related to buying a rice cooker. This complaint from Joo is registered by Hoon and Young in lines 2 through 4 with laugh tokens and Young the complainee produces an apology in line 5. Upon this, Joo's younger brother Hoon issues another complaint toward Young in lines 7 and 8, *way tto kyelhon yayki-lul hay-se tto wuli nwuna-lul tto kentuly-e tto:* ("Why again do you talk about marriage again and so irritate my sister aga:in?"). This utterance is grammatically designed as a question and literally asks for the reason why Young brought up the issue of marriage and irritated his sister. However, in the sequential environment where Young's target behavior has already been complained about and Young herself has apologized, there should not be reasonable grounds that Young could provide to defend her comment. Also, since Hoon's seeming question already defines Young's conduct as "irritating," it does not actually ask to present justification for her act but does a complaint with an assertion that "you should not have talked about marriage again and irritated my sister." In this complaint in which Hoon characterizes Young's act as undesirable, he utilizes the adverb *tto* ("again"). Its use formulates the target act as not only undesirable but also repetitive and intensifies the legitimacy of his claim based on the highlighted repetitiveness. An interesting aspect of using the adverb *tto* in this case is that it is used as many as four times in one grammatical sentence. The repeated uses of the same adverb *tto* gives an extreme emphasis on the repetitive aspect of the target act, which allows the complainant to greatly intensify his claim of complainability.

2.2.5. Summary

This section has explicated how intensifying expressions are used in complaints to strengthen the claims of complainability. Utilizing such intensifying expressions is a strategy that the complainants employ to fortify the grounds of complaining and hence make their complaints more convincing. Thus, the deployment of intensifying expressions in complaints is an interactional strategy which the speakers make the most of in trying to expand the scope of their personal dissatisfaction regarding the target event to a socially shared dissatisfaction.

Formulating absence, deficiency, excessiveness, or unacceptability out of a certain phenomenon and emphasizing those particular aspects are similar to the practice of "highlighting" that Goodwin (1994) discusses in his study on discursive practices used by members of a profession. He defines highlighting as a practice of making specific phenomena in a complex perceptual field salient by marking them in a certain fashion. That is, participants cast their perception of a specific phenomenon into the public domain through the practice of highlighting, and the highlighting practice "structures others' perception by reshaping a domain of scrutiny so that some phenomena are made salient, while others fade into the background" (628). Perception is not, then, a purely mental process restricted to individuals, but is a social phenomenon constituted by social interactants through their interaction. It is what social participants practically achieve while they display and manage their orientations to the ongoing activity. Since social interaction is inherently involved in the way we see the world, socially sharing perception of a certain action as complainable is achieved by interactional contingencies, such as the responses of the complainees. (See 4.2 and 4.3 for discussions on how the complainees respond to the versions of complainability proposed by the complainants, how the complainants in turn react, and thereby how the participants jointly manage the complaint talk and constitute socially accountable phenomena in the ongoing interaction.)

NOTE

1. Its correct spelling is *eykyey* or *aykyay*, but it is often simplified in pronunciation as in Fragment (5) and misspelled as in Fragments (21) and (23).

Chapter 3

Linguistic Resources in Complaints

This chapter examines linguistic resources employed in complaints in Korean. It first explicates devices that are frequently used to initiate complaints. Then, it examines recurrent sentence types and the way in which the particular sentence types operate to do complaining. It also investigates particular kinds of final intonation often utilized in complaints in spoken interaction. While I discuss these linguistic resources in separate sections, it does not mean that these devices are discrete sets of resources which are necessary and/or sufficient to do complaining. Instead, I argue that whether or not those devices can be utilized to do complaints only depends on what other resources are methodically employed, in what interactional contexts they are used, what kinds of actions have been done in the prior contexts, and so on. That is, their status as a resource for complaining can only be achieved depending on all the details of the particular context. Thus, through the detailed analysis of actual examples, this chapter aims to show that the significant status of certain grammatical, lexical, and prosodic formats is achieved only when they are situated in social contexts, and further that linguistic structures and social interactional practices are deeply interrelated.

3.1. RESPONSE CRIES

Korean complaints are found to be recurrently preceded by response cries. Response cries are non-lexical exclamatory tokens such as "wow" or "oops" in English. They are not completely lexicalized expressions and have no grammatical connections to the other elements of the sentence but perform an action of expressing the speaker's emotion or feeling by "externaliz[ing] a presumed inner state" (Goffman 1981, 89). Whereas the functions of response cries are explained within a speaker's individual, psychological inner state from Goffman's perspective, Goodwin (1996, 393) considers their occurrences "as social phenomena that provide very powerful resources for shaping the perception and action of others." The response cries in Korean complaints are found to create the relevance between the target event and the upcoming action of complaining. The relevance is clear especially in spoken interaction in which complaining is done directly toward an addressee. That is, a response cry produced immediately after a target conduct in conversation makes obvious that the speaker's forthcoming utterance is going to be aimed at that particular behavior. These response cries themselves convey the speaker's dissatisfied state despite their non-lexical status and thereby project the upcoming utterance to do complaining (or challenging, blaming, and the like). In some cases, they perform complaining in and of themselves. The following sections will demonstrate what response cries are frequently used to initiate complaints.

3.1.1. *Eykey*

Let me first begin with *eykey* which the previous chapter has presented. As mentioned earlier, *eykey* is a simplified form from the original, *eykyey* or *aykyay*. It is a response cry because it is a non-lexical exclamatory token which has no grammatical features. However, it has a semantic implication on its own, which distinguishes it from most other response cries that have no semantic characteristics. The implication of *eykey* is that the speaker considers the amount of the target object to be insufficient, and therefore it is recurrently employed in complaints formulated based on insufficiency. Its use in complaints in both oral and written discourse is presented in chapter 2, as re-demonstrated below:

(1) [Pizza Gathering]

1   {(1.5)/ ((Yun, the wife, sees Suh, her husband, put some peeled fruit onto a plate.))}

2 → Yun: 에게: 더 깎어:

   eykey: te kkakk-e:

   "***Eykey:*** peel mo:re!"

3   Suh: 더 깎을 거야:

   te kkakk-ul ke-ya:

   "((I)) WILL peel mo:re!"

Linguistic Resources in Complaints 41

(2) [Instagram Post, www.instagram.com]

에게 겨우 요만큼 주고 그 가격이라니 앞으로 과카몰리는 집에서 걍 해 먹는 걸로~~.

eykey kyewu yo-mankhum cwu-ko ku kakyek-i-lani aph-ulo kwakhamolli-nun cip-eyse kyang hay-mek-nun kel-lo~~.

"***Eykey*** serving only this little at that price! ((I've decided)) to make guacamole just at home in the future~~."

(3) [News Report 1, autotimes.hankyung.com]

"**에게게**! 이게 뭐야" 자동차 번호판 파동 재연

"*eykeykey! i-key mwe-ya*" *catongcha penho-phan phatong cayyen*

"'***Eykeykey***! What is this!' Commotion about Vehicle Registration Plates Recurring"

In the complaint from the wife to her husband in Fragment (1), the wife, Yun, first produces *eykey:* in reaction to the complainable event, the insufficient amount of the fruit. Through the use of this particular response cry, she formulates her noticing of the insufficient aspect, expresses her negative affect as a strong reaction to it, and projects the forthcoming utterance to be related to the insufficiency. In other words, based on its semantic implication, *eykey:* effectively characterizes the triggering event as deficient and hence complainable, and thereupon constructs the basis of the upcoming complaining utterance. Regarding Fragments (2) and (3), each case has a gap between the time of noticing the insufficient aspect of the target event and producing the complaint since a social media posting or a news headline is a written response to a past event, rather than an instant reaction at the very moment. The uses of *eykey* and *eykeykey!* (an emphasized variation of *eykey*) in these cases have an effect of delivering the complaints vividly as if the complainants were reacting to the target events at the actual moment when they cannot help but release their strong, negative reaction because of the serious level of complainable aspects. *Eykey* and *eykeykey!* in these written segments of discourse therefore strengthen the degree of complainability and provide a resource for shaping the audiences' perceptions of the target matters.

3.1.2. *A, Awu, Aywu, Au, Ai, Aiko/Aikwu, Eyi, Ehywu*

In addition to *eykey*, numerous other response cries are commonly employed in complaints in Korean. The other response cries do not have any semantic characteristics on their own unlike *eykey*. Many of fragments in chapter 2 show the usage of some response cries, which are re-illustrated in the following.

(4) [Response Cries, *a, awu, aywu, au, ai, aiko/aikwu, eyi*]

1. **아**... 힘들어요 ㅠㅠ

    ***a*...** *himtul-eyo* ㅠㅠ

    "***A*...** ((it)) is hard ㅠㅠ"

2. ↑**아:우:::**↑ 진짜 또 시작이야

    ↑***a:wu:::***↑ *cincca tto sicak-i-ya*

    "↑***A:wu:::***↑ really, ((you)) are starting ((this)) again"

3. °**아유**° .h 덜 익었잖아. (이거).

    °***aywu***° .h *tel ik-ess-canh-a. (i -ke).*

    "***Aywu*** ((it)) is undercooked, you know. (This one)."

4. **아으** 야 자 이 오바하지 말구 빨리 피자 먹어:::.

    au *ya ca i opaha-ci mal-kwu ppalli phica mek-e:::.*

    "***Au*** hey now, don't do *opa* ((/'go overboard')), but come and eat the pizza already:::."

5. **아이** °이거° 이것들이 진짜 <u>사기</u>들링을 주고 받는 이: (1.0) 나쁜 놈들.

    ai °*i-ke*° *i-kes-tul-i cincca <u>saki</u>tulling-ul cwu-ko pat-nun i: (1.0) nappun nom-tul.*

    "***Ai*** °these°, these guys really, you guys are committing <u>fraud</u> together, the:se (1.0) bad guys."

6. **아이구** 아무리 귀엽다구 해도 식당에서 너무 시끄러운거 아니냐.

    aikwu *amwuli kwiyep-takwu hay-to siktang-eyse nemwu sikkulew-un ke ani-nya.*

    "***Aikwu*** no matter how cute ((the kid)) is, isn't ((he/she)) too loud in a restaurant?"

7. °**에이:** 추잡스러°

    °***eyi:*** *chwucapsule*°

    "°***Eyi:*** ((it)) is disgusting°"

All the examples of shown above are complaints from oral conversation except for 1 and 6 which are from web community posts. The response cries, *a, awu, aywu, au, ai, aiko/aikwu,* and *eyi* are frequently found in both oral conversation and informal written communication. When used in written communication, they can be a resource for expressing the complainant's intense dissatisfaction as if he or she were reacting to the target events in real time. In addition to the response cries presented above, another one, *ehywu,* is recurrently found to be used in complaining in both conversation and informal written communication. The following fragment is an example in the format of web community posting.

(5) [Web Community Post 1, www.todayhumor.co.kr]

어휴 기레기들 또 시작이네

ehywu kileyki-tul tto sicak-i-ney

"*Ehywu* the trashy media are starting ((it)) again"

Some of these response cries seem to be employed not only in complaints but also in actions expressing other emotional states such as surprise or pleasure. However, my data corpus shows a dominant usage of these response cries in actions expressing an unhappy state including complaints. In sample data of two and a half hours of conversation and eighty social media postings, I have found 134 instances of these response cries and only 24 of them are used to display the speakers' satisfied state. Different prosodic features may be a factor, which can be examined in a future study.

3.1.3. *Hel*

Hel is a response cry with the similar functions to those of the response cries presented in 3.1.2. However, *hel* differs from the others in that it started to be used as an Internet slang term in the past decade. At first, it was considered to be a slang word used only by young people for their expression of surprise or dissatisfaction, but it is found to be used by other age groups, too, and its usage is found to be extended to other types of discourse.

The following fragment is an example in which *hel* is employed in a complaint produced by a non-typical slang user. This complaint is posted on a web community whose membership is confined to married women only, which means that the members are at least in their twenties and the majority are in their thirties or higher.

44   *Chapter 3*

(6) [Web Community Post 2, www.missyusa.com]

헐 이번달 전기세 400불 ㅠㅠ 방금 빌 나온거 보고 기절할 뻔 했어요.

hel ipen-tal cenki-sey 400 pwul ㅠㅠ *pangkum pill nao-n-ke po-ko kicelha-l ppen hay-ss-eyo.*

"***Hel*** the electricity bill is $400 this month ㅠㅠ ((I)) just saw it and almost fainted."

The following example shows that the usage of *hel* is extended to written news reports. It is a headline which conveys a critique and a complaint against a government official's conduct at a press conference.

(7) [News Report 2, www.viewsnnews.com]

헐~ 박상기 법무 "질문 안 받겠다," 나홀로 기자회견

hel~ Park Sang-ki pepmwu "cilmwun an pat-keyss-ta," na-holo kica-hoykyen

"***Hel~*** Minister of Law *Park Sang-ki* 'I will not take any questions,' alone at press conference"

The change in the status of *hel* can be seen in many open documents. For example, a news article in 2012 reported its popular usage as a new exclamation token among teenagers and occasionally among people in their twenties and thirties. A website, www.KoreanClass101.com, presented it as a Korean slang of the day with a meaning, "oh my god!" in English in 2014 and explained that it is mostly used by young people. However, it was acknowledged in 2016 by the National Institute of Korean Language (opendict.korean.go.kr) as a legitimate word. Their definition of *hel*, "a response cry expressing surprise or shock," does not note it to be a slang word specific to young people. Although its recognition was in a dictionary project of descriptive language, not in a standard Korean dictionary, an official evaluation of it as a word by the National Institute of Korean Language reflects its status as changed from slang to a common word frequently used as a helpful resource for conducting a complaint in Korean.

3.1.4. *Cham na/Na cham, Com/Ccom*

There are response cries the origins of which are semantically and syntactically different lexical items. *Cham na/na cham* and *com/ccom* are such cases. *Cham* is an adverb meaning "very," and *na* is a first-person pronoun like "I" or "me" in English. The combination of these two words, either *cham na* or *na cham*, is often employed in complaints in conversation and informal written communication, and neither of the two words in such cases contains the original semantic and grammatical features. *Com* also has its origin in an adverb whose semantic meaning is "a little" or "please" depending on the context, but it is frequently used in complaining as a response cry without substantial meaning or a grammatical role. The uses of these response cries in complaints are illustrated below.

(8) [Response Cries, *cham na/na cham, com/ccom*]

1. [www.missyusa.com]

   참 나 스타벅스 커스터마이징도 옛말이군요

   cham na *suthapeksu khesuthemaicing-to yeys-mal-i-kwun-yo*

   "***Cham na*** Customizing service at Starbucks is just an old phrase"

2. [www.twitter.com]

   #나참#마트에서보고저건절대안사야지했는데아빠차에떡하니있는 #허니통통...

   #na-cham#*mathu-eyse-po-ko-ce-ke-n-celtay-an-sa-ya-ci-hay-ss -nuntey-appa-cha-ey-ttekhani-iss-nun#henithongthong...*

   "***#Na-cham*** #When((I))SawItAtAGroceryShop,((I))Swore((I))Would NeverBuyIt, ButThen((I))FoundItRightInMyDad'sCar

   #Henithongthong..."

3. [www.missyusa.com]

   아 정말 이 스캠 **쫌** 어떻게 **쫌**!! 안 뜨게 할 수 없나요?

   *a cengmal i sukhaym **com** ettehkey **ccom**!! an ttukey ha-l swu eps-na-yo?*

   "A seriously this scam ***com*** somehow ***ccom***!! Can't ((you)) do anything, so ((it)) won't show up?"

Regarding Example 3, a response cry, *a*, initiates the complaint, the degree of which is elevated later with the use of another response cry, *com*. The particular practice of using *com* has multiple features highlighting the action of complaining. First, it employs *com* not once, but twice. Second, *ccom* in the second occurrence begins with *cc*, a tense version of *c*. The repetitive uses of the response cry, *com*, and the tensification of the initial consonant in the second use further strengthen the degree of complaining initiated by *a*. In fact, the combination of the two response cries, *a* and *com* (or the intensified version, *ccom*) is frequently employed as one unit in complaints, as presented in the following examples:

(9) [Response Cries, *a com/ccom*, www.twitter.com]

1. 아쯤 인간들아 내 의자 좀 잡지마아 악

    a ccom inkan-tul-a nay uyca *com* cap-ci maa ak

    "*A ccom* you idiots do not grab my chair *com* agh"

2. 아쯤 말 좀 들어 제발 쯤

    a ccom mal *com* tul-e ceypal *ccom*

    "*A ccom* listen *com* please *ccom*"

These examples show not only that *a* and *com/ccom* is utilized as a unit in complaints but also that *com/ccom* can be repeatedly used multiple times within one complaint. Based on such practices, we can see that *com/ccom* is considered to be an effective device for manifesting a dissatisfied emotional state while complaining in Korean.

3.1.5. Summary

This section has shown that response cries are recurrently deployed in complaints in Korean. By openly displaying their negative affect in reaction to a target event through response cries, the complainants gather the participants' attention to certain matters and claim them to be too reprehensible to restrain themselves from releasing a visible cry. Having focused the attention of the participants on the target events through the response cries, the complainants subsequently explicate the complainable features in the actual complaints. The response cries thus play an important role in tying together the complainable events and the actual complaints, impacting the participants' perceptions, and thus bringing the complainants' personal-level dissatisfaction to the public sphere. The deployment of such response cries therefore is an important step to develop the action of complaining as a social activity. Response cries also have an impact on the participants' responses and the structure of the following discourse. Their impacts on the organization of complaints will be discussed in 4.1.

3.2. SENTENCE TYPES

This section describes sentence types that are used in performing complaining in Korean and discusses how those particular syntactic formats are mobilized in complaints. Four sentence types are found to be recurrently employed as grammatical resources in complaining: declaratives, interrogatives with question words, "yes/no" questions, and imperatives. The following discussions describe in what contexts and how these particular types of sentences are used as complaints, and show that the interactional contexts of the sentences and other coordinating resources, rather than the grammatical types themselves, are the key to treating those sentences as complaint utterances.

3.2.1. Declaratives

We have seen declarative sentences deployed in complaints earlier in this book, and some of the examples are re-listed below in (10).

(10) [Declaratives in Complaints]

1. °에이: 추잡스러°

    °*eyi: chwucapsule*°

    "°*Eyi:* ((it)) is disgusting°"

2. 야 오늘 우리 ㄷ-- 다 모여서 고기 구워먹기로 했는데 너만 안 왔어:

    ya onul wuli t-- ta moy-ese koki kwuwe mek-ki-lo hay-ss-nuntey ne-man an wa-ss-e:

    "Hey we have decided to gather for a meat party a-- all together today, but you are the only one who hasn't co:me!"

3. 어휴 기레기들 또 시작이네

    ehywu kileyki-tul tto sicak-i-ney

    "*Ehywu* the trash media are starting ((it)) again"

4. 도대체 언제 갖다 주시나요? **한 시간이 넘었는데. 전화 수십 통을 해도 안 받으시네요.**

totaychey ence kacta cwu-si-na-yo? **han sikan-i nem-ess-nuntey. cenhwa swusip thong-ul hay-to an pat-usi-ney-yo.**

"When in the world are you going to bring ((the food))? **It has been over an hour. ((You)) don't answer the phone even though ((I)) call dozens of times.**"

The declarative format is found in all types of discourse, and it is most utilized in formal written complaints, an example of which is shown in the following.

(11) [Formal Complaint, www.incheon.go.kr]

1 제목: 신고해도 처리해 주지 않는 쓰레기

   sinkohay-to chelihay cwu-ci ahn-nun ssuleyki

   Title: "Trash not taken care of although it was reported"

2 10월 1일 무단으로 쓰레기를 투기하고 간 차량이 cctv에 찍혀

   10-wel 1-il mwutan-ulo ssuleyki-lul thwukiha-ko kan chalyang-i cctv-ey ccikhy-e

3 신고하였습니다. 그런데 오지 않아 추후 두번이나 더 확인

   sinkohay-ess-supnita. kulentey o-ci anh-a chwuhwu twu-pen-ina te hwakin

4 전화를 하였습니다. **그런데도 아직도 오지 않네요.**

   cenhwa-lul hay-ess-supnita. **kulentey-to acik-to o-ci anh-ney-yo.**

5 **쓰레기는 여전히 집앞에 있는데도 말입니다.**

   ssuleyki-nun yecenhi cip-aph-ey iss-nuntey-to mal-i-pnita.

"A car which disposed trash without permission was caught on CCTV on October 1st, and ((I)) made a report. However, no one came, and therefore ((I)) made two more phone calls to make sure. **Even after that, no one has come yet. No one has even though the trash is still in front of ((my)) house.**"

This is a complaint asserting that the city government did not follow up on trash pickup, although it was reported multiple times. The complaint begins in the title as a noun phrase and develops more details in the main body. The last two declarative sentences in the main body performs the action of complaining due to the lack of a proper response from the city.

While declarative sentences are often employed in complaints in all types of discourse, complaining assertions are regularly delivered in phrasal form as well, especially in social media postings and titles of written discourse including news articles and formal complaints. An example is seen in the title of Fragment (11) above, and more instances are listed below:

(12) [Phrases in Complaints]

1. [Space Heater Review, www.coupan.com]

    완전 가까이에서만 따뜻

    wancen kakkai-eyse-man ttattus

    "Warm only when ((I)) am completely close"

2. [Hotel Review, www.tripcoupang.com]

    최악~~ 윗층 층간 소음 화장실 배수도 잘 안되고

    choiak~~ wis-chung chung-kan soum hwacangsil payswu-to cal an toy-ko

    "The worst~~. The noise from upstairs. The bathroom water not draining well, either."

3. [News Headline, autotimes.hankyung.com]

    "에게게! 이게 뭐야" **자동차 번호판 파동 재연**

    "*eykeykey! i-key mwe-ya*" ***catongcha penho-phan phatong cayyen***

    "'*Eykeykey*! What is this!' **Commotion about Vehicle Registration Plates Recurring**"

The declarative format is used for complaining with the help of various other resources such as response cries and lexical items which formulate the different types of complainability discussed in chapter 2, rather than with the help of the declarative sentence type itself. The next sections present interrogatives and imperatives as significant syntactic resources which contribute to performing complaints more from their sentence types themselves than the declarative format.

3.2.2. Interrogatives with Question Words Conveying Reversed Polarity Assertions

Interrogative sentences with question words are commonly utilized in complaints. Although they are grammatically formatted as questions, these sentences do not seek new information as real questions, but convey reversed polarity assertions, which convey the complainant's stance of negatively evaluating and thus being dissatisfied with the target event. These questions have been explicated regarding their interactional usage among English speakers in earlier research: Koshik (2003, 2005) has called these types of questions reversed polarity questions or RPQs,[1] since they convey assertions of the opposite polarity to that of the question, and discussed that such RPQs are useful resources for challenging the recipient's prior behavior or utterance in interaction Korean interrogatives with questions words regularly operate as RPQs in complaining as well, and some are taken from prior examples and presented below.

(13) [Interrogatives with Question Words in Complaints]

1. **왜** 일부러 말들을 안 하구 그래:. ((laugh)) .h

   WAY ilpwule mal-tul-ul an ha-kwu kulay:. ((laugh)) .h

   "**WHY** are ((you guys)) intentionally not saying anythi:ng? ((laugh)) .h"

2. >**무슨**< 유세를 해요: 한꺼번에 저렇게 다 갖구와가지구:

   >*mwusun*< *ywusey-lul hay-yo: hankkepeney celehkey ta kackwuw-akacikwu:*

   "**What** arrogance did ((I)) sho:w? ((You)) brought all the materials at once like tha:t"

3. **어찌** 내가 전활 안 하면 전활 한 통화도 안 하냐?

   ecci nay-ka cenhwa-l an ha-myen CENHWA-L HAN THONGHWA-TO an ha-nya?

   "**How come** ((you)) NEVER MAKE A SINGLE PHONE CALL ((to me)) if I don't call ((you))?"

4. 딸 키우시는 엄마분들... 이 짓을 **언제**까지 하나요? ㅠ

   ttal khiwu-si-nun emma-pwun-tul... i-cis-ul encey-kkaci ha-na-yo? ㅠ

   "Those of you moms who raise daughters... **How long** should ((I)) do this stupid thing? ㅠ"

The following example illustrates how such RPQs perform complaining. We have seen Fragment (14) before in which Young complains toward her roommate at a dinner gathering which they are hosting together. Young's complaint in line 1 is formulated in a *way* ("why") question.

(14) [Dinner Talk among Five Friends]

((Young comes to the table and looks into the stew pot. Then she grabs a plate with a vegetable and puts some into the stew.))

1 → Young: *더 많이 늫지: **왜 요만큼 넜대:***

   *te manhi nuh-ci: **way yo-mankhum ne-ss-tay:***

   * *: ((keep putting vegetable into the stew))

   "((You)) should've put mo:re. **Why did ((you)) put this litt:le?**"

2   {(0.5)/ ((Young keeps putting vegetable into the stew.))}

3   Young: 이쁨-- 이쁨만 강조했구나.

   ippum-- ippum-man kangcohay-ss-kwuna.

   * *: ((keep putting vegetable into the stew))

   "Pretti-- ((you)) were just emphasizing the pre:ttiness ((of it)), right."

The first sentence in line 1, *te manhi nuh-ci:* ("((You)) should've put mo:re ((vegetable into the stew))"), displays the speaker's belief and expectation that the amount of the vegetable should have been larger. Her normative expectation is targeted at the recipient's preceding conduct of putting a particular amount of vegetable into the stew and thus becomes the yardstick with which the target conduct is assessed. The utterance thus implicitly performs a negative assessment claiming that the recipient cooked an insufficient amount of vegetables and at the same time challenges the target behavior.

The action of negatively assessing and challenging the target behavior is more clearly done through the sentence, *way yo-mankhum ne-ss-tay:* ("Why did you put this litt:le?"). Although the linguistic format of this sentence is an interrogative with a question word, the sequential environment makes it heard not as an information-seeking question, but a challenge and thereby a complaint directed at the preceding target behavior. That is, in the preceding context, the speaker has expressed her expectation about a certain behavior on the recipient's part and declared that the target performance was below her expectation. The speaker has thereupon established the context of negatively assessing the target performance and expressing her dissatisfaction with it. The *way*-question in this context makes the recipient's performance accountable by asking her to justify putting in such a small amount of vegetables. However, since Young has already established her expectation about the amount as a normative standard in the preceding sentence, it implies that the target behavior of putting in a particular amount of the vegetable is not justifiable and the *way*-question is thus not answerable. That is, the preceding sentence defines the target conduct as unjustifiable, and the following *way*-question implies that the recipient will not be able to provide a reasonable answer. Therefore, the sequential environment makes the *way*-question heard as a negative assertion, "There is no good reason for you to put in so little," rather than an information-seeking question. This utterance formulates the target conduct as a failure to reach the cooking standard which Young has set up, and thus it performs a challenge and a complaint.[2]

As seen in this example, interrogative sentences with question words are recurrently used as complaints in Korean. These interrogatives function as complaints in the context where a certain normative standard has been set up as a yardstick with which the complainant assesses the target conduct or event as some kind of failure for the particular situation. These interrogatives convey assertions instead of asking real questions. The assertions display the speakers' strong epistemic stances and thereby perform complaints which claim that the target behavior has violated the normative standard.

The type of interrogatives with question words seems to be particularly grammatically and interactionally useful for making complaints, especially toward the addressee. A question is usually used as a first pair part of an adjacency pair (Sacks 1992),[3] which requires an answer as its second pair part. However, an RPQ in a complaint does not necessarily require an answer since it is not an information-seeking question, and even makes an implication that there is no proper ground for the addressee's action, that is, no acceptable answer. On the other hand, the question still opens a complaint sequence as a first pair part and interactionally makes relevant the addressee's response: The addressee is called upon directly to defend an action which the complainant has already characterized as norm-violating. Whereas a simple declarative like "You should have put more" can do the work of challenging an action, the RPQ is stronger because it leads toward an interactional demonstration of the complainee's culpability. If the complainee fails to produce an adequate second pair part, an acceptable reason for the complained-about behavior, that failure can be seen as proof of guilt. Since the interrogative complaint format makes relevant the addressee's response, and, at the same time, implies that the addressee will not be able to reasonably answer the question, it sets the complainee up for interactional failure. Therefore, the grammatical format and the interactional pressure become resources by which the complainant creates the failure of the addressee and formulates the target conduct as unacceptable.

3.2.3. "Yes/No" Interrogatives Conveying Reversed Polarity Assertions

The analysis of complaints in Korean reveals that "yes/no" questions are also used as a useful linguistic resource in all types of discourse. Just as interrogatives with question words do, "yes/no" questions convey reversed polarity assertions as opinions and function as complaints in particular sequential contexts, rather than asking for information. Such functions of "yes/no" RPQs as challenges or complaints have been examined in earlier research in different settings of oral interaction in English (Heritage 2002; Koshik 2005), and earlier fragments in this book have shown cases in Korean. The following examples are some of them.

(15) ["Yes/No" Interrogatives in Complaints]

1. 전화를 받아야 주문을 하지 않을까요?

   cenhwa-lul pat-aya cwumwun-ul ha-ci anh-ulkka-yo?

   "Isn't it that ((I/we)) can place an order only if ((you)) answer the call?"

2. 아이구 아무리 귀엽다구 해도 식당에서 너무 시끄러운거 아니냐.

   aikwu amwuli kwiyep-takwu hay-to siktang-eyse nemwu sikkulew-un ke ani-nya.

   "*Aikwu* no matter how cute ((the kid)) is, isn't ((he/she)) too loud in a restaurant?"

3. 이 자식들. .h 나한테 그 연락 하나 못 하냐?

   I CASIK-TUL. .h NA-HANTHEY KU YENLAK HANA MOS HA-NYA?

   "THESE JERKS. .h ((YOU)) COULDN'T EVEN CONTACT ME?"

4. 야 결혼 안 하면 맛있는 거 먹으면 안 돼?

   ya kyelhon an ha-myen masiss-nun ke mek-umyen an tway?

   "Hey if not married, can ((we)) not eat delicious food?"

To understand how "yes/no" interrogatives operate as an effective resource for complaining, I will examine the sequential context of Example 4 above, *ya kyelhon an ha-myen masiss-nun ke mek-umyen an tway?* ("Hey if not married, can ((we)) not eat delicious food?"). It is taken from a conversation at a dinner gathering which Young and Jeong are hosting for their friends. Fragment (16) below is an extended segment. In the prior discourse to this fragment, the participants were talking about electronic pressure rice cookers. Young said that she could not buy one because of its high price. Joo, a guest, then insisted that an electronic pressure rice cooker is worth buying. In response, Young says in lines 1 and 2 in the following excerpt that it would not be necessary anyway because she would not have any chance to get married soon. As a cultural background of this utterance, there is an expectation that when Korean people get married, the bride brings appliances and furniture while the bridegroom takes care of the housing. Young makes this cultural expectation relevant to her utterance in lines 1 and 2, which asserts that she would not need to buy an expensive rice cooker soon because she does not have any chance to get married while she is staying in the United States for her graduate study. With this utterance, she implies that she might need to wait until she gets married when she goes back to Korea after finishing her studies in the United States to buy one.

(16) [Dinner Talk among Five Friends]

1   Young: ↑그↑ 뭐 어차피: 여기에 안-- (0.5) 뭐 여기서: 뭐 (0.5) 결혼할

　　　　　　　↑ku↑ mwe echaphi: yeki-ey an-- (0.5) mwe yeki-se: mwe (0.5) kyelhonha-l

2   　　　　　일도 없는데 뭘 좋은(h) 걸(h) 사(h) ((chuckle))

　　　　　　　il-to eps-nuntey mwe-l cohun(h) ke-l(h) sa(h) ((chuckle))

　　　　　　　"↑That↑ uh here ((I)) don't-- (0.5) uh he:re uh (0.5) there isn't even any chance ((for me)) to get married here ((/in the US)), and then why would ((I)) buy(h) a good(h) one(h) ((chuckle))"

3   Jeong: ((chuc[kle))

4   Young: [((laugh))

5   (.)

6   Jeong: 결혼(은) <여기서> 결혼해서 여기서 같이 살지도 모르죠:,

　　　　　　　kyel(hon)-un <yeki-se> kyelhonhay-se yeki-se kathi sa-l ci-to molu-cy-o:,

　　　　　　　"Getting married <here>, it can be possible ((for you)) to get married and live here with ((your husband)), you know"

7   (0.5)

8 →Joo: 야 결혼 안 하면 맛있는 거 먹으면 안 돼?

　　　　　　　ya kyelhon an ha-myen masiss-nun ke mek-umyen an tway?

　　　　　　　"Hey if not married, can ((we)) not eat delicious food?"

Young's utterance in lines 1 and 2 is first heard as a joke through her laugh token, which makes another recipient, Jeong, respond with a chuckle in line 3. Jeong also treats Young's utterance as a self-deprecation, which implies that she does not see a chance of getting married in the near future. Jeong disagrees with Young in line 6 by claiming that it is possible for Young to get married in the United States, meaning "soon" because it is where she is right now. Jeong's disagreement in this context is a preferred response to Young's self-deprecation (Pomerantz 1984). Joo's earlier suggestion that Young buy a nice rice cooker has then transformed into Young's cultural normative orientation that single women do not need to buy nice appliances until they have specific wedding plans, and Jeong aligns with this normative orientation. It is at this point of the talk when Joo issues a "yes/no" question in line 8, *ya kyelhon an ha-myen masiss-nun ke mek-umyen an tway?* ("Hey if not married, can ((we)) not eat delicious food?"). Based on the preceding context, this utterance is clearly heard as an assertion displaying her opinion rather than an information-seeking question, despite its grammatical format. First, Joo's suggestion of buying a nice rice cooker was targeted toward Young, who is single. Therefore, Joo's original stance was that anybody, married or not, can buy their own deluxe rice cooker. Young then rejects the assertion, making clear her position that the rice cooker is too expensive for her to buy without any prospect of getting married in the near future. Joo's utterance in this context of displaying positions is thus heard as a disagreeing opinion statement that "we can eat delicious food even if we are not married," which adheres to her original position. Joo's utterance further challenges Young's stance and complains by bringing up the relevance of Young's normative standard to her personal background. Joo is a single woman who is several years older than Young. According to Young's sociocultural orientation shown in the preceding context, Joo could be considered to have wasted money on buying an expensive rice cooker even without getting married. Joo's utterance makes visible this consequential interpretation of Young's normative orientation and thereby complains toward Young's act of raising the issue of marriage related to buying a rice cooker.

Reversed polarity "yes/no" questions seem to have grammatical and interactional advantages, as interrogatives with question words do, to be used as complaint utterances over the corresponding assertions. The complainant in the example above could have issued an assertion, "we can still eat delicious food even if not married," instead of the reversed polarity question, "Hey, if not married, can we not eat delicious food?" However, the reversed polarity question not only expresses the speaker's opinion as the corresponding assertion but also sequentially makes relevant, as the first pair part, the addressee's response as the second pair part. The RPQ, then, puts the addressee in an interactional "tight spot," where he or she is called upon to answer a question

56 Chapter 3

to which the strongly implied answer is a clear admission of guilt. The reversed polarity questions therefore enable the complainants to challenge and complain toward the addressees' target conduct or utterances more effectively than the corresponding assertions.

3.2.4. Imperatives

Imperative sentences are another type of grammatical resource for complaints, especially when they target the addressee directly. The imperative is a sentence type, which is often used to perform a command or a request. Since a command or a request is a demand that the recipient do something that has not been done yet, or stop doing the current action, the format of imperative sentences is useful for pointing out the complainee's failure to do an expected action or an improper aspect of his or her current action. Some examples from earlier fragments are listed below.

(17) [Imperatives in Complaints]

1. 아쫌 말 좀 들어 제발

    a ccom mal com tul-e ceypal ccom

    "*A ccom* listen *com* please *ccom*"

2. 에게: 더 깎어:

    eykey: te kkakk-e:

    "*Eykey:* peel mo:re!"

3. 아으 야 자 이 오바하지 말구 빨리 피자 먹어::.

    au ya ca i opaha-ci mal-kwu ppalli phica mek-e::.

    "*Au* hey now, don't do *opa* ((/'go overboard')), but come and eat the pizza already::."

Let me explain in detail how an imperative sentence becomes a useful resource for complaining in an actual interactional context. In Fragment (18) below, Min, a guest at the social dinner gathering, complains to another guest, Won, who is not participating in the dinner activities because he is working on a Lego construction.

(18) [Pizza Gathering]

((Won working on Lego construction, and everybody else gathered at table))

1   Suh: °이따 만들어: 먹구:°

              °*itta mantul-e: mek-kwu:*°

              "°Make it la:ter After ea:ting°"

2   ((several turns deleted: Won keeps working on Lego construction))

3 → Min: 아으 야 자 이 **오바하지 말구 빨리 피자 먹어::**.

              au ya ca i ***opa-ha-ci mal-kwu ppalli phica mek-e::***.

              "*Au* hey now, **don't do *opa* ((/'go overboard')), but come and eat the pizza already::**."

4   Won: °이게 더 재밌어요::.°

              °*i-key te caymiss-eyo::.*°

              "°This is more fu:n.°"

The complaint utterance in line 3 consists of two imperative clauses, which are connected in a similar way to the English structure, "don't do A, but (instead do) B." The first imperative clause, *opaha-ci mal-kwu* ("don't do *opa*") characterizes Won's ongoing conduct as *opa* ("going overboard"). The expression *opa* refers to an act of doing something to a greater extent than is reasonable as discussed in 2.1.3, and this particular lexical choice formulates Won's act as inappropriate. This formulation of the current target act as improper is contrasted with the second imperative clause, *ppalli phica mek-e::*. The second imperative clause expresses what Won should do as a remedy and thereby declares that Won has been doing something which needs to be stopped and rectified.

Other resources are also utilized to formulate Won's target act as complainable. The adverb *ppalli* ("right away") in the second imperative clause describes it as an inadequate behavior which needs to be remedied immediately, in other words, too inappropriate to wait further. Also, the final intonation adds a blaming quality to the utterance. The intonation represented by the two underlined colons (::) following the transcription convention used in conversation analytic methodology (Ochs et al. 1996) indicates that there are two occurrences of inflected rising intonation at the end of the utterance. Such an inflected rising intonation, which will be further discussed in the next section, is often found in complaint utterances in Korean. The intonation in this segment helps the imperative utterance implicitly deliver an assertion, "You should've joined us earlier," in an accusing tone. Through the practices of emphasizing that Won's current act needs to be immediately stopped and remedied, specifying its inadequate feature as going overboard, and conveying accusation with the particular final intonation, Min's utterance consisting of two imperatives characterizes Won's behavior as a failure to be a proper social participant and performs a complaint against it.

While the imperative format is instrumental in pointing out the lack of an expected action or the inadequacy of the current action, the imperative format itself is not intrinsically related to complaints. As the analysis above has shown, a variety of other linguistic and paralinguistic resources highlighting the inappropriateness of the target conduct enable the imperative utterances to do complaining. Therefore, the action of complaining is done only when all the grammatical, lexical, and paralinguistic resources are coordinately employed to highlight undesirable aspects of target conduct.

3.2.5. Summary

This section examines the sentence types which are often utilized in complaints in Korean. It has found that interrogatives with question words, "yes/no" questions, and imperatives are recurrently employed in complaining. The two types of questions investigated in this section are not real information-seeking questions. Instead, they are challenges and complaints which convey opposite polarity assertions and thereby display the complainants' negative stances toward the target behavior. These types of questions create an interactional complication which the complainees have to handle: They open complaint sequences as first pair parts and interactionally make relevant the complainees' responses, and at the same time, are constructed in a manner that discourages the complainees from "answering the questions" by conveying the complainants' strong assumption that the complainees will not be able to give answers which can defend their behavior. Therefore, the grammatical formats and the interactional pressure become resources by which the complainants formulate the target conduct as complainable. The imperative sentences are also instrumental in pointing out the lack of an expected action or inappropriateness of the complainees' current action, which the complainants consider needs to be remedied. Thereupon, the complainants' formulation of the target act as complainable can be created and the complaining action can be done.

However, the grammatical resources can function to do complaining only when they cooperate with other resources which formulate a certain target act complainable in relation to the particular participant(s) and the particular moment in the ongoing interaction. The grammatical types examined in this section are not inherently related to the complaining action. Rather, they can operate as complaints only when they are situated in interactional contexts, which suggests that grammar is only one set of resources for accomplishing a task within a social event, and that the organization of grammar and that of social interactional practices are deeply interrelated.

3.3. LATER UPWARD INTONATION

The analysis of complaint utterances in Korean talk-in-interaction has uncovered recurrent uses of a particular type of final intonation contour. For example, of the twenty oral complaints presented thus far in this study, eleven complaint utterances involve a recurrent final intonation pattern represented by an underlined colon (:), a transcription symbol used for an inflected rising intonation in conversation analytic methodology (Ochs et al. 1996). Some of them are represented in the following:

(19) [Recurrent Final Intonation in Complaints]

1. 왜 일부러 말들을 안 하구 그래:.

    WAY ilpwule mal-tul-ul an ha-kwu kulay:.

    "WHY are ((you guys)) intentionally not saying anythi:ng?"

2. 왜 또 결혼 얘기를 해서 또 우리 누나를 또 건드려 또:

    way tto kyelhon yayki-lul hay-se tto wuli nwuna-lul tto kentuly-e tto:

    "Why do you again talk again about marriage again and so irritate my sister aga:in?"

3. 무슨 유세를 해요: 한꺼번에 저렇게 다 갖구와가지구:

    >mwusun< ywusey-lul hay-yo: hankkepeney celehkey ta kackwuw-akacikwu:

    "What arrogance did ((I)) sho:w? ((You)) brought all the materials at once like tha:t"

4. 아으 야 자 이 오바하지 말구 빨리 피자 먹어::.

    au ya ca i opa-ha-ci mal-kwu ppalli phica mek-e::.

    "*Au* hey now, don't do *opa* ((/'go overboard')), but come and eat the pizza already::."

5. 야 오늘 우리 ㄷ-- 다 모여서 고기 구워먹기로 했는데 너만 안 왔어:

    ya onul wuli t-- ta moy-ese koki kwuwe mek-ki-lo hay-ss-nuntey ne-man an wa-ss-e:

"Hey we have decided to gather for a meat party a-- all together today, but you are the only one who hasn't co:me!"

Ochs et al. (1996, 464) explain that "if a colon is itself underlined, then there is an inflected *rising* intonation contour (i.e., you can hear the pitch turn upward)." In other words, an underlined colon indicates an upward inflection while the vowel is being stretched. The target intonation contour in my Korean data, however, needs further elaborations, especially in comparison with the rising intonation symbolized with "?". Whereas "?" indicates an intonation contour in which rising occurs from the beginning of the final syllable, ":" means that the final syllable begins with a low flat intonation, and then an upward inflection occurs *after* the final syllable has started. These two intonation contours can be schematically represented with a lengthened final syllable *-e:* as in figure 3.1.

Since an upward inflection occurs later than in the regular rising intonation, I call this intonation contour "a later upward intonation." I have found a later upward intonation sometimes followed by a final falling intonation (indicated as ":."). The later upward intonation is sometimes extended with another or more upward inflections, as seen in Example 4 above (:::.). These variations are schematically represented in figure 3.2.

No matter how it ends, or no matter how long the final vowel is stretched, the later upward inflection is frequently observed in complaint utterances in my Korean conversation data. Intonations of this type parallel a group of final intonations identified by Jun (2005), who has developed a transcription framework for Korean prosody known as the Korean Tones and Break Indices (K-ToBI). In the framework of K-ToBI, an intonation phrase (IP) is marked by a boundary tone (%) at the end and final lengthening. The boundary tone is realized in the IP-final syllable, and nine boundary tones have been identified depending on the shape of contour starting from the onset of the final

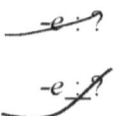

Figure 3.1 Regular Rising Intonation versus Later Upward Intonation. *Source*: Figure courtesy of the author

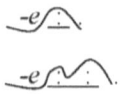

Figure 3.2 Variations of Later Upward Intonation. *Source*: Figure courtesy of the author

syllable. They are L%, H%, LH%, HL%, LHL%, HLH%, HLHL%, LHLH%, and LHLHL%, with L and H symbolizing "low" and "high," respectively. The difference between H% and LH% is explained in terms of the timing of the rising: LH% rises later than H%. The group of IP-tones beginning with LH (LH%, LHL%, LHLH%, and LHLHL%) correspond to the variations of later upward intonation I have identified. The K-ToBI, briefly recognizes a function of most of the LH-prosodic group as signaling annoyance or irritation, and this function is related to the action of complaining which has been explicated in this book.

The later upward intonation group (or the LH-prosodic group) is not, however, intrinsically associated with the complaining action. This intonation becomes a resource for complaints only when other coordinating resources and sequential contexts contribute to constructing environments in which complaints are relevant. For example, the later upward intonations are employed in complaint utterances with interrogatives with question words in Examples 1 through 3 in (19). As discussed in 3.2.2, these types of questions call into question the ground of the complainee's previous action and convey the complainant's strong position that there is no adequate reason for the target act. Hence, the interrogatives become powerful resources to do complaints, and the later upward intonations do not seem to distinguish these types of questions specifically as complaining but to intensify the quality of complaining. In the imperative and declarative complaint utterances, in which the sentence types themselves do not have as much effect in constructing complaints as the interrogatives, the later upward intonations play a greater role.

To see how this particular intonation operates as a resource for complaints, let's look at examples with and without the later upward intonations and compare them with each other. First, let me present examples of utterances in the imperative format without a later upward intonation.

(20) [Family Lunch]

((Wife, Husband and his sister is having spaghetti lunch together.))

1 → Wife: *이거 **먹어.**

*i-ke **mek-e.**   *((putting meatball onto Sister's dish))

"**Eat** this."

(21) [Beer Gathering] (Slightly simplified)

((Three friends, Hyun, Jin, and Koo, are having a beer gathering. In the immediately preceding talk, Jin said he did not feel comfortable in his stomach.))

62   *Chapter 3*

1   Koo: 속 거북한데 (0.6) 고기를 뜯어 먹으면 안 되°잖아.°

             sok kepwukha-ntey (0.6) koki-lul ttute mek-umun an toy-°cy-anh-a.°

             "((toward Jin)) Since ((you)) don't feel comfortable in your stomach (0.6) ((you)) should not eat the beef jerky, right."

2 → Hyun: 이거 이거 **먹어:.** 음:? *칩에다 이거 해서.*

             *i-ke i-ke **mek-e:.** u:m? *chip-eyta i-ke hay-se.**

             * *: ((dipping chip into salsa))

             "((toward Jin)) This, **ea:t** this. Oka:y? Chips with this ((/salsa))"

The imperative utterances, *i-ke mek-e.* and *i-ke k-ke mek-e:.*, in the fragments above are an offer and a suggestion from the speakers to the addresses: The wife in Fragment (20) offers a meatball to her sister-in-law, and Hyun in Fragment (21) suggests to his friend that he try another kind of food instead of beef jerky because his stomach is bothering him. Each of these utterances consists of a verb (*mek-e*, "eat") and an object (*i-ke*, "this") without other linguistic resources, and employs the common final falling intonation. The two speakers' physical actions contribute a lot to indicating that they are making an offer and a suggestion through the short, simple utterances, but if they used a later upward intonation, the utterances would not be heard as an offer or a suggestion. The following fragment involves a short imperative utterance with the same verb, *mek-e*, but conveys a complaining tone by employing a later upward intonation.

(22) [Pizza Gathering]

((A married couple, Yun and Suh, are having a pizza gathering with three other friends in their home. The participants have been eating and talking for about 30 minutes. Suh, the husband, sees Yun talking without having not finished eating yet.))

1 → Suh: °**먹어:**°

             °*mek-e:*°

             "°**Ea:t**°"

2   (0.5)

3   Yun: 먹구 있잖아 계:속, 먹는데 왜 그래?

             <u>mek</u>-kwu iss-cy-anh-a kyeyso:k, mek-nuntey way kulay?

"((I)) am eating, conti:nuously! Why do ((you)) say that although ((I)) keep eating?"

Suh's utterance in this example does not have any other resource in the turn, which could build an action, except for the verb in the imperative format produced with a later upward intonation. This turn design is very similar to those of the imperative utterances in (20) and (21), which function as an offer and a suggestion. The most substantial difference of Suh's utterance from the ones in (20) and (21) is the final intonation. The later upward intonation in Suh's utterance thus plays an important role in expressing his dissatisfaction about Yun's act of talking too much instead of finishing eating. The addressee, Yun also displays the orientation to Suh's complaining and accusing action, by responding to him with a complaint, "((I)) am eating, conti:nuously! Why do ((you)) say that although ((I)) keep eating?" If she had heard Suh's utterance as an offer or a suggestion, she would not have responded with a complaint.

However, the example of Suh's utterance does not necessarily show that the imperative utterance performs a challenge only through the later upward intonation. In this case, the context in which the utterance is produced plays a great part in making it do a challenge. In the prior discourse approximately 20 minutes before Fragment (22), Suh has already challenged Yun by saying, *phica mek-e: ne mwe ha-nya?* ("Eat pizza: What are you doing?"). Suh's next imperative utterance with the same verb which is targeted toward the same addressee, Yun, and the same object, pizza, thus cannot be heard as a favorable invitation to eat food. Instead, it functions as persistent pressure to make Yun eat, and at the same time, a challenge against the non-eating behavior by Yun. Therefore, the construction of the challenging action depends, to a large extent, on the particular context in which the utterance is issued, as well as the specific type of utterance and the intonation.

The later upward intonation, in cooperation with the sequential environment and other turn constructional resources, plays a significant role in forming the complaint action with declarative utterances as well as with imperatives. The following segment shows an example. We have seen this segment in earlier sections focusing on the analysis of Yun's complaint, but we will now pay attention to Suh's response in the declarative format in line 3.

(23) [Pizza Gathering]

1   {(1.5)/ ((Yun, the wife, sees Suh, her husband, put some peeled fruit onto a plate.))}

2   Yun: 에게: 더 깎어:

    eykey: te kkakk-e:

    "*Eykey:* peel mo:re!"

3 → Suh: **더 깎을 거야:**

    te kkakk-ul ke-ya:

    "**((I)) WILL peel mo:re!**"

The earlier analysis has demonstrated that Yun's turn in line 2 is a complaint conducted about the deficient amount of fruit, consisting of a response cry, an imperative, and a later upward intonation. In response, Suh issues a counter-challenge in line 3. If he aligned with Yun's notice of the amount of the fruit as insufficient, he would have issued an acceptance token such as "ok," "yeah," or "I see." Instead, he declares without any hesitation that he will peel more, which displays his attitude misaligning with Yun's complaint. He then expresses his emphatic upset state through a later upward intonation, which makes the utterance a counter-complaint.

Now I will show how the particular intonation makes the utterance display the speaker's emphatic upset state and thereby do a counter-complaint, by presenting another example similar to Fragment (23), but without the same intonation. The following is an earlier portion than Fragment (22). We have seen that Suh has done a challenge against Yun regarding her current act of talking too much instead of eating. Line 4 is Yun's response to this challenging and scolding:

(24) [Pizza Gathering]

((In the immediately preceding talk, Yun chatted with one of the guests, Yeon.))

1   ((Yun keeps talki[ng))]

2   Suh: [피]자 먹어: 너 뭐하냐?

                    [*phi*]*ca mek-e: ne mwe ha-nya?*

                    "Eat pizza: What are you doing?"

3   (0.8)

4 → Yun: 음 먹으께 떠든다구:.

um mek-ukkey *tte*tu-nta-kwu:.

"Yes, ((I)) will. Because ((I)) was busy tal*k*ing too: much."

The sequential position of Yun's response in line 4 is the same as the one in which Suh's is produced in Fragment (23): Both are issued after the prior speakers have challenged the current speakers' behavior. The sentential design of Yun's response in this segment is also very similar to that of Suh's in (23): Both are declaratives ending with the similar sentence ending suffixes, *-ukkey*, a colloquial variation of *-ul-key*, in Yun's response and *-ul-keya* in Suh's, both of which function like "will," an English modal verb. The two responses hence differ in that Yun's declarative utterance is preceded by an acceptance token *um* ("yes") and does not end with a upward later intonation whereas Suh's in (23) does not employ an acceptance token, but the upward later intonation.

Regarding the sequential context in Fragment (24), Suh's challenge in line 2 has created a contesting environment in which counter-challenging could be a next relevant action by the recipient. However, Yun instead displays her aligning position with Suh's challenge and complies with his command through the use of the acceptance token and the lack of later upward intonation. Her complying position is further evidenced through her subsequent turn, *ttetu-nta-kwu:*. ("Because ((I)) was busy tal*k*ing too: much."). In this turn, she gives an account of why she has not been eating, and in doing so, she herself characterizes her target act as inappropriate by using the verb *ttetu* ("make a noise") with a negative connotation, even with a stress on the first syllable.

In comparison with Yun's complying response, we can see in Fragment (23) how the lack of an acceptance token and the employment of a later upward intonation play a critical role in making Suh's declarative utterance do a challenge and a counter-complaint. By not producing an acceptance token, Suh displays his misaligning attitude toward Yun's command. Furthermore, the use of a later upward intonation manifests his emphatic upset state as well as his misaligning attitude. That is, the particular prosody attaches to the statement an implication that he is irritated by Yun's order because he has no need of it and he himself knows how to prepare fruit for the guests. Suh's utterance is thus not a simple statement that he will peel more fruit, but a strong action of complaining that Yun treats him as a disrespectful host who does not even know how to serve guests. In this way, Suh utilizes the later upward intonation as a critical resource for formulating a counter-complaint.

This section has demonstrated that later upward intonation contours are useful resources to formulate and/or intensify complaint utterances in Korean. The findings in this book thus provide corroborating evidence, based on actual occurrences found in natural conversation, for previous research such as Jun (2005) which claims that those particular intonation contours are used to express annoyance or irritation. However, I have also argued that later upward intonations are not intrinsically related to actions of complaining or challenging. Later upward intonations can be a resource for complaints only when other coordinating resources are jointly employed, and/or when they are used in sequentially complaining-relevant contexts.

3.4. SUMMARY

To summarize, this chapter has illustrated what kinds of linguistic resources are employed and how they work in complaints in Korean. It has shown that response cries are useful resources for openly reacting to the triggering event with negative affect and thereby claiming the target act to have remarkably inappropriate features which make the complainant release a visible cry. The inappropriate features of the target act are explicated in the actual complaints, in the format of declaratives, interrogatives with questions words, "yes/no" questions, or imperatives. According to the observation of the ways in which the grammatical, lexical, and prosodic resources are used in complaints, these resources and the sequential contexts of the turns can neither be put in a specific order with regard to which resource is more primary than another, nor separately explained in terms of their roles in creating the action. Instead, all of them jointly operate to perform complaining based on their intertwined relationship, demonstrating that grammatical shapes of language are built through its situated uses to perform certain social actions during the course of interactional discourse.

NOTES

1. Line 28 shows an example ("when have I.") from Koshik (2003, 52):

((Two friends, Debbie and Shelley, are having an argument. Debbie has accused Shelley of pulling out of anpcoming trip together because her boyfriend cannot go.))

```
26    Debbie:   =I do'know,=jus don't blow off your girlfriends for
27              guy:s, Shel.
```

28 → Shelly: De:b I'm not. h[ow man-]e- when have I.=beside ya-
29   Debbie: [o k a : y]

2. Suh (2004) discusses various interactional functions of *way*-utterances in non-interrogative contexts, including complaint-related actions: She finds that *way*-utterances are used for expressing recognition, criticism, challenge and exclamation as well as filling in a necessary interactional space.

3. See Sacks (1992, 521–569) as a major resource on the adjacency pair.

Chapter 4

Organization of Complaining Activity

The previous chapters have focused on what a complainant does within a complaint turn and how he or she does so. This chapter examines how a complaining activity is organized at the initial stage, how it is developed to a response to the complaint, and how it is closed with or without further expansion afterward. It first explicates the initial stage in which participants engage themselves in a projected complaining activity. It moves to investigating recurrent patterns of responses to complaints and then the subsequent turns. Since this volume examines both direct and indirect complaints, the range of possible response types is very wide and the subsequent turns can be developed in a multitude of ways. Although it is insurmountable to provide a complete account of all of them, this section presents some recurrent ways in which a complaining activity is organized. Through the analysis of the organizational features of a whole complaining activity from the initial stage to the closing, this chapter aims to show how complainants and recipients interactionally manage coordinated actions throughout the course of the activity.

4.1. INITIAL STAGE: RESPONSE CRIES AS ORGANIZATIONAL RESOURCE

The previous chapter illustrated that complaints are recurrently preceded by response cries in Korean. The response cries usually occur after a triggering event formulated later as complainable, and before some complaining comments on the event, as demonstrated in the following.

{Triggering Event} → {Response Cry} → {Complaint}

Since they are non-lexical sounds which have no syntactic relation to any other element, "the way in which they indicate what they are responding to is through adjacent positioning and immediate juxtaposition" (Goodwin 1996, 394). That is, the response cries, through the sequentially adjacent location, establish the relevance between the triggering event which has happened in the immediately preceding context and what the speaker is going to do next. The importance of the response cries is that they display "the sudden, immediate and spontaneous character of the actor's reaction to the triggering event" (Goodwin 1996, 395) and cast the triggering event as powerful enough to cause the actor's unthinking release of his or her affective status. By releasing his or her spontaneous negative reaction in the visible cry, the complainant characterizes and frames the preceding event as some kind of a failure to meet a proper normative standard in the particular context.

Not only do the response cries characterize the triggering event as a failure but they also project the forthcoming remark to be related to the complainable feature of the triggering event. Thereby, they provide the recipient with an interpretational framework for the upcoming explicit complaint and make him or her ready to coordinately respond to the complaint in the ongoing complaining activity. In the cases of direct complaints, the response cries operate as a resource for retroactively positioning the addressee, who is the actor of the triggering event, as a complainee and for preparing him or her to respond to the projected complaint accordingly. That is, they invoke a participation framework which makes particular types of next actions (e.g., an apology or a counter-complaint) relevant to that complainee in the complaining activity.

Let me explain this through Fragment (1) in the following, in which Min complains toward his friend, Won, because Won treated him with "so much arrogance" when he asked for a favor.

(1) [Pizza Gathering] (Slightly Simplified)

1 Yun: 사층에 계속 계셨어요?

sa-chung-ey kyeysok kyeysy-ess-eyo?

"Did ((you)) stay on the fourth floor for a long time?"

2 (1.0)
3 Min: 아니 뭐 찍는 거 부탁하느라구

ani mwe ccik-nun ke pwuthakha-nulakwu

"Well uh because ((I)) needed to ask ((Won)) a favor, some help with Measuring"

| 4 → | *아이구:[: 저 인간 유]세하는 거 때문에 내가 아주, |

aikwu:[: *ce inkan ywu*]*seyha-nun ke ttaymwuney nay-ka acwu,*
* ((Min's eye-gaze changing from Yun to Won. Also, moving his head forward a little while producing *aikwu::*, as if he were striking Won with his head.))

"*Aikwu::* because that human being (((/a despicable expression of 'person')) was showing so much arrogance, I was so like"

| 5 → Won: | [↑아유::↑] |

[↑*aywu::*↑]

"↑*Aywu::*↑"

| 6 | Won: | >무슨< 유세를 해요: 한꺼번에 저렇게 |

>*mwusun*< *ywusey-lul hay-yo: hankkepeney celehkey*

| 7 | | 다 갖구와가지구: hu |

ta kackwuw-akacikwu: hu

"What arrogance did ((I)) sho:w? ((You)) brought all the materials at once like tha:t hu"

Min's complaining action begins in line 4 with the preface *aikwu::*. In the following utterance, Min elaborates what event has led him to release the response cry: By referring to Won as *ce inkan* ("that human being"), which holds a connotation that the party referred to is in some way despicable, and characterizing what Won did to him as "showing so much arrogance," he makes clear that the triggering complainable event was Won's unpleasant treatment of him when he asked for help. Min's complaint in this case is directed toward an event that occurred several hours before, not in the immediately preceding context. That is, while response cries usually react to the events in the instant setting, *aikwu::* in Min's utterance is a reaction to the event at a distant time. It is nevertheless employed to show its relevance to the triggering event although it is distant. The response cry is produced immediately after Min says that he went to Won because he needed to ask for help, which happens to be the background situation for the complainable event. This explicit mention of the background in the directly preceding talk provides *aikwu::* with the sequential basis for its relevance to the triggering event. Moreover, Min, who has been looking at Yun while he is answering her in line 3, directs his eye-gaze toward Won exactly when he begins to produce *aikwu::* and gestures toward Won by moving his head forward a little. Thereby, he manifests that his response cry is drawn out in reaction to Won's triggering behavior. Based on the sequential basis, the eye-gaze, and the gesture, *aikwu::* indicates that a complainable event occurred at the time of his visit to Won and also that the complainable feature was so strong that it still elicits an involuntary, exclamatory reaction from him at this moment.

The mechanism of the response cry is very powerful in this talk-in-interaction and thus it instantly positions Won as a complainee, which is visible through his reaction: He produces his own response cry ↑*aywu::*↑ in line 5 in response to Min's *aikwu::*. Won starts to issue this response cry while Min is elongating the final syllable of the response cry *aikwu::*. This is even before Min starts to explain what exactly he has responded to with *aikwu::* and what he is going to complain about. Nonetheless, Won displays, by deploying ↑*aywu::*↑ at the particular moment, that he has noticed both the events which have triggered Min's *aikwu::* and the course of action which Min is carrying out. That is, Min's *aikwu::* effectively operates as an important instrument in both manifesting the relevance of the triggering complainable event to the forthcoming action, and projecting the forthcoming action of complaining in this particular context.

As for Won's response cry ↑*aywu::*↑, it projects and indeed leads to his counter-complaint toward Min's complaint (lines 6 and 7, >*(mwusun)*< *ywusey-lul hay-yo: hankkepeney celehkey ta kackwuw-akacikwu:* "What arrogance did ((I)) sho:w? ((You)) brought all the materials at once like tha:t"). Won's counter-complaining action is hence done in the same way as Min's complaint. The whole procedure of the complaining activity between Min and Won also follows the same pattern. That is, the complainant issues a response cry triggered by a complainable event, and continues to do a main complaint. The complainee reacts with his own response cry prefacing a complaint and proceeds to a counter-complaint. The procedure of this activity between the two parties is demonstrated in figure 4.1.

What needs to be noted here is that the activity is not organized in a linear way. In other words, the two parties' actions are overlapped significantly in the course of the activity instead of their turns being allocated one after the other. The overlap in this talk has the ground of its occurrence in the complaining actions that are being carried out at the particular moment: As discussed above, Min's *aikwu::* indicates that he is initiating a complaint toward Won's earlier conduct, and Won displays his noticing of it through ↑*aywu::*↑ as early as possible, with an overlap from the terminal point of *aikwu::* through the middle of the subsequent complaint utterance. Won launches his counter-complaint at this early stage because it is the point in which Min's complaint has only been projected but not yet explicated, and hence Won can still prevent Min from proceeding to the main part of the complaining. Min however advances his complaint in an overlap with Won's

{Triggering Event by Complainee Won}
↓

Complainant Min: *aikwu:*[: + 저 인간 유]세하는 거 때문에 내가 아주,
    'Because that human being was showing so
    much arrogance, I was so like'

Complainee Won: [↑*aywu:↑*] + >무슨< 유세를 해요:
    한꺼번에 저렇게 다
    갖구와가지구:
    'What arrogance did ((I)) sho:w?
    ((You)) brought all the materials
    at once like tha:t'

{Triggering Event by Complainee Won}
↓

Complainant Min: *aikwu:*[: + {C]omplaint}
Complainee Won: [↑*aywu:↑*] + {Counter-complaint}

Figure 4.1 Complaining Activity Organized through Response Cries. *Source:* Figure courtesy of the author.

response cry. Won makes another attempt later to stop Min's complaint with an interruption. When Min begins to deliver his explanation of the emotional impact of Won's complainable act (*ce inkan ywuseyha-nun ke-ttaymwuney nay-ka acwu*, "Because that human being was showing so much arrogance, I was so like"), Won issues his own counter-complaint and blocks grammatical completion of Min's utterance.

In brief, the complaining activity in this fragment is shaped through the intertwined co-participation from both the complainant and the complainee in a very finely tuned manner, and the response cries operate as highly effective resources all through the procedure. The highly interactive procedure demonstrates that complaining is a socially coordinated activity between multiple participants rather than a unidirectional action. In this procedure, the response cries play a critical role in creating the relevance between separate parties' actions as well as between different parts of one party's action. The response cries thus enable the participants to perform a particular type of action which is coherently connected to the other party's relevant action at an appropriate moment.

The practice of using response cries at the onset of complaints is often observed in informal written communication as well. The following examples are postings on Instagram and Twitter which are complaints initiated by response cries.

74   *Chapter 4*

    (2) [Response Cries in Written Complaints]

    1.   [Instagram Post, www.instagram.com]

        #**아이씨** #연습 #더럽게안되네

        *#**ai-ssi** #yensup #telepkey-an-toy-ney*

        "#***Ai-ssi*** #Practice #HorriblyGoingWrong"

    2.   [Twitter Post, www.twitter.com]

        #**에잇~!!** #당연한것을질문하는것을우문이라합니다

        *#**eyis~!!** #tangyenha-n-kes-ul-cilmwunha-nun-kes-ul-wumwun-i-la-ha-pnita*

        "#***Eyis~!!*** #AskingAnObviousQuestionIsCalledAStupidQuestion"

Example 1 is an Instagram posting with a dance practice video and Example 2 is a Twitter posting with a Retweet questioning a political figure's behavior. As noted in chapter 3, a social media posting is a written response to a past event, rather than an immediate reaction at the very moment, and therefore there is a gap between the time of noticing and the complainable aspect of the target event and producing the complaint. A response cry in such a case establishes the relevance between the past event and the complaint posting and delivers the complaint vividly as if the complainant was reacting to the target event at the actual moment. The two response cries used in these social network postings thus play as resources for shaping the audiences' perceptions of the following remarks and the contents of the video clip and the Retweet which are posted together.

In sum, a response cry helps complainants openly display their negative affect in reaction to a target event, gather other participants' attention, and claim the target event to be too reprehensible to restrain themselves from releasing a visible cry. Having focused the attention of the participants on a particular event, they subsequently explicate the complainable feature in the actual complaint turn. The power of a response cry is sometimes so strong that it draws out other participants' reaction on its own even before the projected complaint is actually issued. In this way, the response cry ties together the complainable event and the complaint utterance, forms the participants' perception, and prepares them to respond to the projected complaint accordingly. Such roles of a response cry are reflected in the organization of a complaining activity from its initial position to the following main complaint and to the recipients' response in the subsequent turn sometimes with overlapping. A response cry thus plays an important role in coordinating the interactive activity of complaining as a social phenomenon.

4.2. SEQUENCING IN DIRECT COMPLAINT ACTIVITY

Sequencing in conversation refers to the ways in which turns are initiated, responded, and combined to make actions take place in interactions (Schegloff 2007). Examples of sequencing practices are sequences of question-answer, offer-acceptance/decline, request-comply/reject, and the like. Jefferson (1988) notes that interactants have been repeatedly instructed on the proper procedures of ritualized sequences such as greetings and question-answer sequences, and there are known consequences for not doing what ought to be done. She further notes that it may be unreasonable to demand a strictly ordered progression except for those ritualized small sequences. Complaint sequences are not as tightly organized as the ritualized small sequences, either. A reason for such loose organizations of complaint sequences may be that possibly relevant response types have a wide range. Although it is difficult to provide a complete account, this section presents some general patterns of responses to direct complaints and further development of the sequences after the responses.

4.2.1. Responses to Direct Complaints— Acknowledging Complainability

As discussed in chapter 2, complaints are constructed through characterization of the target event as unacceptably absent, insufficient, excessive, or present. Complainees in direct complaints respond with various actions including apologies, account-giving, counter-complaints, and so on. Through these various actions, the complainees admit or deny that their conduct is complainable. In my data corpus, they acknowledge the complainability by apologizing or account-giving. When they deny the complainability, they do so in two ways. On the one hand, they acknowledge the occurrence of the target event, but deny its wrongdoingness. On the other hand, they deny the occurrence of the target event itself and counter-complain.

When complainees respond to the complaints in a way that they acknowledge the blameworthiness of their conduct, they do so by apologizing or giving an account. Fragment (3) in the following excerpt shows an example of apologizing. It is a conversation among five friends at a dinner gathering. In the preceding talk, Young has raised the issue of marriage related to buying a rice cooker and brought up a sociocultural norm that single women do not need to buy nice appliances until they have a certain wedding plan. Then Joo, who is a single woman but has purchased an expensive rice cooker, complains about and challenges Young's stance in line 1. (See (16) in 3.2.3. for the preceding talk and the discussions on how Joo's utterance does complaining.)

(3) [Dinner Talk among Five Friends]

1	Joo:	야 결혼 안 하면 맛있는 거 먹으면 안 돼?

ya kyelhon an ha-myen masiss-nun ke mek-umyen an tway?

"Hey if not married, can ((we)) not eat delicious food?"

2	Hoon:	((ch[uckle))
3	Young:	[((chuckle)) ((l [a u g h))]
4	Hoon:	[((chuckle))]
5 →	Young:	**미안해** s:: ((laugh))

mianhay s:: ((laugh))

"((I)) **am sorry** s:: ((laugh))"

Hoon and Young register Joo's complaint with laugh tokens (lines 2 through 4). Then, Young the complainee produces an apology in line 5, through which she acknowledges that her conduct was inappropriate and complainable.

Fragment (4) is another example where the complainee apologizes in response to a complaint. It is a segment drawn from the conversation among close friends at a pizza gathering Suh and Yun host. To provide more background information, the guests arrived earlier than Yun and have been waiting for her. In the immediately preceding context to this fragment, Yun has just arrived. In line 1, she greets Min, one of the guests, who is the oldest participant.

(4) [Pizza Gathering]

1	Yun:	*안녕하세요. 이발 또 하셨네요,=

**annyengha-sey-yo. ipal tto ha-sy-ess-ney-yo,*=

*: ((bow at Min))

"How are you? ((/literally, 'Are you well?')) ((You)) got a haircut again,"=

2	Min:	=안녕 못 하다.

=*annyeng mos ha-ta.*

"((I)) can not be well."

3	Yun:	왜요:.

way-yo:.

"Why:."

| 4 | Min: | 니가 늦게 와가지구.= |

          ni-ka nuckey w-akacikwu.=
          "Because you came late."

| 5 → | Yun: | =.h 죄송합니다:. haha .h *↑죄송합니다↑ .h |

          =.h *coysongha-pnita:.* haha .h *↑*COYSONG*ha-pnita*↑ .h
                                   *: ((take a deep bow))
          =".h ((I)) am sorry:. haha .h ↑((I)) am SORRY↑ .h"

In line 1, Yun greets Min and recognizes his new haircut, too, which makes two responses expected in Min's turn. However, neither does he return greeting to Yun nor respond to Yun's notice of his haircut. Instead, he treats Yun's greeting as a real question, answers to the literal meaning of the ritualistic greeting expression, and declares that he is not well (line 2). Then he provides, as an answer to Yun's follow-up question, the reason of why he is not well: He says that he "cannot be well" because Yun is late for the gathering (line 4). This atypical response to a common greeting functions as a strong complaint about the host's late arrival. Yun responds to this complaint with an apology in line 5. She produces an apology, *coysongha-pnita:* ("((I)) am sorry"), in a formal, deferential speech style, and then reproduces it as an upgraded one, with the use of high pitch, loud voice, and a gesture of bowing. In this way, the complainee clearly accepts the inadequacy of her action and cooperatively participates in constructing the complainability of the target conduct.

In the following fragment, the complainee also acknowledges, by giving an account, that her conduct was not adequate. At the same time, however, she claims it to be explainable through the account and thereby tries to reduce the degree of the blame laid on her. This fragment is a conversation between two female roommates who are hosting a dinner gathering, and the two hosts are cooking a stew.

(5) [Dinner Talk among Five Friends]

((Young comes to the table and looks into the stew pot. Then she grabs a plate with a vegetable and puts some into the stew.))

| 1 | Young: | *더 많이 늫지: 왜 요만큼 넜대:* |

          **te manhi nuh-ci: way yo-mankhum ne-ss-tay:*
          * *: ((keep putting vegetable into the stew))
          "((You)) should've put mo:re. Why did ((you)) put this litt:le?"

2   {(0.5)/ ((Young keeps putting vegetable into the stew.))}
3   Young: 이쁨-- 의쁨[만] 강조했구나.

ippum-- ippum[-ma]n kangcohay-ss-kwuna.

* *: ((keep putting vegetable into the stew))

"Pretti-- ((you)) were just emphasizing the prettiness ((of it)), right."

4 → Jeong: [반--]

[pan--]

"Half--"

5   {(.)/ ((Young keeps putting vegetable into the stew.))}
6 → Jeong: 반씩 (.) 이따 (넣을)라구.

pan-ssik (.) itta (neh-ul)lakwu.

"Half (.) ((I)) was gonna put the other half later."

Line 1 is a complaint about Jeong's cooking performance based on characterization that the amount of the vegetable which she has put into the stew as insufficient. In responding to this complaint, Jeong explains the reason she has put that particular amount of the vegetable. The account is that she was going to put the other half later, and she admits through this account that the amount she has put in was indeed insufficient and hence complainable. However, she simultaneously justifies her target conduct as a result of having an intention to put the other half later, claiming that she shares the same cooking standard as Young and that she was going to fulfill the standard with a necessary amount at a later stage. Formulating a justification in this way is the complainee's attempt to reduce blame in managing the complaint issued toward her.

The complainees in Fragments (3), (4), and (5) agree with the complainants on the inadequacy of their behavior. From the ethnomethodological point of view, complainants cast their personal perception of inappropriateness into the public domain through complaints. Then, we can view that complainees' responses acknowledging the inadequacy affirm the complainants' perception. Thus, when the complainees admit the problematic feature of their conduct through apologizing or giving an account, they join the complainants and collaboratively construct complainability.

Such responses from the complainees also imply that they affirm normative standards that have been proposed through the original complaints. As mentioned in the preceding chapter, complaints involve proposing certain normative standards. For example in Fragment (3), Young proposes a particular sociocultural norm that single women do not need to buy expensive appliances until they have a specific wedding plan. Another participant Joo, who recommended to her that she buy an electronic pressure rice cooker, then contests it through a complaint, *ya kyelhon an ha-myen masis-nun ke mekumyen an tway?* ("Hey if not married, can ((we)) not eat delicious food?"). Joo's complaint suggests an alternative orientation, that anybody, whether or not married or planning to get married, can buy a nice rice cooker for their own sake. This alternative version is affirmed by Young through her apology, and it is thereupon constituted as a socially shared orientation between the two participants through their complaining activity. In Fragment (4) as well, the complainant suggests a norm that the host should not be late for the gathering and make the guests wait. The complainee shows the same orientation to the norm by apologizing. The participants in Fragment (5) also propose and affirm, through their complaint and account, a cooking norm that they should put in a particular amount of vegetable to make tasty the particular type of stew they make. Therefore, when the complainees agree on the complainability, they also affirm normative standards proposed through the original complaints and thereby co-participate in constructing normative standards for the local contexts.

4.2.2. Responses to Direct Complaints—Denying Complainability

Now we move to the responses which deny the complainability constructed by complainants. The analysis of my data reveals two ways of denying the complainability. On the one hand, complainees acknowledge the occurrence of the target event but disagree about the wrongdoingness of the target event. On the other hand, they deny the occurrence of the target event itself and often issue a counter-complaint as well.

Let me first present responses which disagree on the wrongdoingness of target events. Fragments (6), which is taken from the pizza gathering, shows an example. In this fragment, Min complains against Won because Won would not stop working on Lego construction, although all the other participants are waiting for him to eat together. Line 2 is Won's response to the complaint.

(6) [Pizza Gathering]

((Won working on Lego construction, and everybody else gathered at table))

1   Min: 아으 야 자 이 오바하지 말구 빨리 피자 먹어::.

         au ya ca i opa-ha-ci mal-kwu ppalli phica mek-e::.

"*Au* hey now, don't do *opa* ((*l'*'go overboard")), but come and eat the pizza already:::."

2 → Won: °이게 더 재밌어요:.°

°*i-key te caymiss-eyo:.*°

"°**This is more fu:n.**°"

Min's complaint is done in combination with a request which makes compliance or refusal relevant a response. Won responds with a protesting final intonation (see 3.3 for discussions on later upward intonation) and state that playing with the Lego toy is more fun to him. While and after he produces the response, he does not show any gestural sign of stopping building the Lego construction but keeps working on it. His utterance and physical orientation display his determination not to comply with the request, and at the same time give an explanation of why he is not complying. In this way, he acknowledges that he is doing the action of "not joining the others because of playing with the toy" but denies that his conduct is wrongdoing, through the account that playing with the toy is more entertaining.

The complainee in Fragment (7) below also acknowledges his target action but rejects its reprehensibility. This segment is from a conversation among three male roommates in their early twenties. Hoy has stayed at home all day and Jo just came home for dinner. In line 1, Hoy tells Jo that he watched a Korean TV show called "All In" while Jo was out. In this announcement, Hoy displays his excitement about the show through loud voice quality. In response, Jo says that he will also watch it on the following day (line 3). Hoy expresses his enthusiasm about the show again (line 5), and after a pause, Jo issues a complaint initiated with a response cry *au* (line 7). In this complaint, Jo brings up their earlier promise to watch it together, and thereby defines as a breach of promise Hoy's act of watching it while Jo was away. Hoy's response in line 9 to this complaint is a challenge against the accusation.

(7) [Roommate Talk] (Slightly simplified)

1   Hoy: 올인 봤다:.

ALL IN PW-ASS-TA:.

"I WATCHED ALL I:N."

2   (2.2)

3   Jo: 한꺼번에 두 편 내일 봐야지.

hankkepeney twu phyen nayil pw-aya-ci.

"Two episodes at a time, ((I)) will watch tomorrow."

4   (3.2)
5   Hoy: 어:으 진짜 재밌어.

              e:u cincca caymiss-e.
              "*E:u* ((it)) is really stunning."

6   (1.8)
7   Jo: °아으: (혼자) 보냐 같이 보° °°(기로 해놓고.)°°

              °*au: (honca) po-nya kathi po*°- °°*(ki-lo hay-noh-ko.)*°°
              "°*Au:* how could ((you)) watch it (without me)? After ((we)) decided° °°to watch it together.°°"

8   {(1.5)/ ((Jo looks at Hoy))}
9 → Hoy: **하루종일 뭐 할까.**

              halwucongil mwe ha-l-kka.
              "What would ((I)) do all day long then?"

Hoy's response to Jo's complaint in the format of "what"-question conveys an assertion that there is nothing else to do while he stays home all day long. In this utterance, Hoy portrays the time that he stays at home as *halwucongil* ("all day long"), which is a maximized expression of *halwu* ("a day"). Such a formation emphasizes the lengthiness of the time he stayed at home and provides an excuse for doing what he wants to do to pass the time. He also forms the utterance with the prospective modal suffix *-l*, the basic meaning of which is probability or predictability (Sohn 1999, 361). Since this utterance, as well as the original complaint utterance, targets Hoy's past behavior, a past tense suffix could have been used to refer back to it. However, Hoy instead uses the prospective modal suffix with the meaning of predicting possibilities, and thereby extends the target of his utterance from a particular act that he did at a particular time to what he would usually do in other similar situations. Using these lexical and grammatical resources, he claims it to be generally justifiable to watch an entertaining video if he has a great amount of time to spend. Based on this justification, he challenges Jo's complaining position and rejects the accusation while admitting that he watched the show alone despite his earlier promise with Jo.

The complainees in Fragments (6) and (7) disagree with the complainants about the wrongdoingness of their target conduct and thereby deny the complainability. Another way of rejecting complainability is to deny the occurrence of the target event itself. In many cases, in which complainees employ this strategy, they not only reject the complainability but also counter-complain against the original complainants. Fragments (8) and (9)

82   *Chapter 4*

show such examples. In Fragment (8), the wife complains against her husband regarding the amount of fruit he has chopped for the gathering, and the husband responds with a counter-complaint.

(8) [Pizza Gathering]

1   {(1.5)/ ((Yun, the wife, sees Suh, her husband, put some peeled fruit onto a plate.))}

2   Yun: 에게: 더 깎어:

   eykey: te kkakk-e:
   "Eykey: peel mo:re!"

3 → Suh: 더 깎을 거야:

   te kkakk-ul ke-ya:
   "((I)) WILL peel mo:re!"

The wife's original complaint is done in the form of a request. It requests her husband to peel more fruit, and at the same time points out the amount of the fruit peeled as insufficient and complains that he has prepared only a deficient amount of food for the social gathering. In response, the husband claims that he will peel more, from his own decision. His claim implies that Yun's judgment that he has put a stop to the job is thus wrong, and that the complained-about conduct, which is preparing too little fruit, has not occurred. By arguing that the job is still ongoing, he invalidates the ground of the request and rejects the complaint. In addition, he further constructs his utterance as a counter-complaint by implying a challenge, "you didn't have to tell me that!," through the later upward intonation which expresses his emphatic upset state.

In Fragment (9) as well, the complainee denies the occurrence of the complained-of conduct and at the same time counter-complains against the first complainant. It is the segment in which Min accuses Won of treating him with so much arrogance. In response to Min's complaint, Won projects his discontent with a response cry in line 5 and subsequently issues a counter-complaint saying that it was Min who had brought too many materials to handle at one time.

(9) [Pizza Gathering] (Slightly Simplified)

1   Yun: 사층에 계속 계셨어요?

   sa-chung-ey kyeysok kyeysy-ess-eyo?
   "Did ((you)) stay on the fourth floor for a long time?"

2   (1.0)
3   Min: 아니 뭐 찍는 거 부탁하느라구

ani mwe ccik-nun ke pwuthakha-nulakwu

"Well uh because ((I)) needed to ask ((Won)) a favor, some help with measuring"

4   아이구:[: 저 인간 유]세하는 거 때문에 내가 아주,

aikwu:[: ce inkan ywu]seyha-nun ke ttaymwuney nay-ka acwu,

"*Aikwu::* because that human being ((/a despicable expression of 'person')) was showing so much arrogance, I was so like"

5   Won: [↑아유::↑]

[↑ *a y w u :: ↑*]

"↑*Aywu::*↑"

6 → Won: >무슨< 유세를 해요: 한꺼번에 저렇게

>*mwusun*< *ywusey-lul hay-yo: hankkepeney celehkey*

7 →   다 갖구와가지구: hu

ta kackwuw-akacikwu: hu

"What arrogance did ((I)) sho:w? ((You)) brought all the materials at once like tha:t hu"

The first sentence in line 6, >*(mwusun)*< *ywusey-lul hay-yo:* ("What arrogance did ((I)) sho:w?"), is designed as an interrogative with "what," to convey an assertion that he did not show any arrogance at all, and thereby to completely deny the accusation. Not only does it deny the accusation, it also carries out complaining: In this contesting environment that Min's earlier complaint has already established, a challenge would be a relevant next action and a reversed polarity question (RPQ) is especially likely to be interpreted as a challenge (Koshik 2003). Won's RPQ indeed operates as a challenge, and the use of the later upward intonation upgrades the challenging quality of the utterance. Moreover, with the second sentence, *hankkepeney celehkey ta kackwuw-akacikwu:* ("((You)) brought all the materials at once like tha:t"), Won brings everybody's attention to the amount of materials that Min brought for help. This second sentence immediately follows the RPQ whose meaning is "I didn't show any arrogance!," and characterizes the amount as inappropriately excessive for a session of help. In this way, it maximizes the contrast between Won's claim about his innocence and Min's action of bringing too many materials and claims Min's behavior, not his own, to be complainable. That is, he completely denies the alleged behavior, and further counter-complains against the original complainant.

Fragment (10) presents a similar response in written communication. It is a response to a formal complaint posted on a local government's website. The complaint is regarding the absence of cracking down on unlicensed tour guides' business, and the person in charge responds with a denial of the alleged lack of the government's enforcement.

(10) [Formal Complaint, www.jeju.go.kr]

Complaint:

안녕하십니까? 한국인 중국어 가이드입니다. ((several sentences omitted)) 아울러 무자격 가이드에 대한 단속을 강화해야 합니다. 제주도에서 많이 다녔어도 저는 단속하는 모습을 아직 보지 못 했습니다.

annyengha-si-pnikka? hankwukin cwungkuke kaitu-i-pnita. ((several sentences omitted)) *awulle mwucakyek kaitu-ey tayhan tansok-ul kanghwa-hay-ya ha-pnita. ceycwuto-eyse manhi tany-ess-eto ce-nun tansokha-nun mosup-ul acik poci mos hay-ss-supnita.*

"Hello? ((I)) am a tour guide for Chinese speakers. ((several sentences omitted)) In addition, ((you)) should strengthen a crackdown on hiring the unlicensed guides. ((I)) go around a lot on Jeju Island, but ((I)) have not seen any crackdown on ((them))."

Response: ((beginning parts omitted))

무자격 관광안내 행위 단속은 매년 실시하고 있으며, 특히 올해는 '17년 예산 (80백만원) 대비 50% 증액(120백만원)하여 지난 1월부터 월 2회 단속을 시행하여 왔으며, 금년 32건의 단속건에 과태료를 부과하였습니다. 남은 기간동안 단속을 더욱 더 철저하게 단속을 추진하여 무자격자 근절을 위해 노력하도록 하겠습니다.

mwucakyek kwankwang-annay hayngwi tansok-un maynyen silsiha-ko iss-umye, thukhi olhay-nun '17 nyen yeysan (80 paykman-wen) taypi 50% cungayk(120 paykman wen)ha-ye cinan 1 wel-pwuthe wel 2 hoy tansok-ul sihayngha-ye wa-ss-umye, kumnyen 32 ken-uy tansok-ken-ey kwathaylyo-lul pwukwaha-yess-supnita. *nam-un kikan-tongan tansok-ul tewuk te chelcehakey tansok-ul chwucinha-ye mwucakyekca kuncel-ul wihay nolyekha-keyss-supnita.*

"**((We)) enforce cracking down every year on tour guide conduct by the unlicensed. Especially this year, ((we)) have a budget of 120 million won which is increased 50% from last year (80 million won). Based on it, ((we)) have conducted the enforcement twice a month since last January**

and have imposed fine on 32 cases of violations. ((We)) will continue the enforcement more strictly and thereby try to completely stop the violations of the unlicensed."

The complainant alleges, based on his personal observation, a lack of the governmental oversight to enforce the law. The respondent counter-claims that they do enforce cracking down, and thereby denies the allegation about the lack of government control. In so doing, the respondent provides specific data on how they conduct the particular job in question. The provision of the information validates the respondent's claim and strengthens the position of denying the complainability. At the same time, it plays a role of the public service which is different from the practices found in ordinary conversation like Fragments (8) and (9). Since it is a response to a formal complaint toward a government, it does not accompany a counter-complaint but instead plays a role of serving citizens by informing them.

We have seen how complainees deny the complainability constructed by complainants. They do so by either disagreeing about the complainability while acknowledging the occurrence of the target event, or denying the occurrence of the target event itself, sometimes counter-complaining at the same time. In these ways, complainees refuse to participate in co-constructing complainability with the complainants and simultaneously negotiate normative standards for the particular contexts.

4.2.3. Responses to Direct Complaints—Summary

This section has demonstrated how complainants and complainees cooperatively construct certain conduct as complainable when the complainees acknowledge the inadequacy in their responses (4.2.1.1), and how the target conduct is not established as a transgression between the two parties when the complainees reject the complainability in their responses (4.2.1.2). When the complainees acknowledge the complainability, they also agree with the complainants' normative orientations. In cases where the complainees deny the complainability, they sometimes affirm or sometimes contest the other party's normative orientations. For example, in Fragment (6), in which the complainee is accused of not participating in eating together, the complainant displays his sociocultural orientation that every participant should join in beginning the meal altogether for a harmonious social gathering. The complainee, however, contests it and presents his own norm, which is that he does not have to join in if he finds something else more entertaining. On the other hand, the complainee can reject the complaint but affirm the norm proposed by the complainant as in Fragment (8). In this fragment, the complainant suggests a norm that the hosting

86   *Chapter 4*

party of a social gathering should provide a sufficient amount of food to the guests. Although the complainee challenges and counter-complains against the original complainant, he shows the same orientation to the norm in his response saying that he will prepare more. In the government's response in (10) as well, the respondent denies the complainability, but expresses a strong position that the government office has the same norm against the unlicensed tour guides' business.

The complaining activity also involves the process of shaping the perception of certain phenomena in specific ways. As noted by Goodwin (1994) and mentioned in the preceding chapter of this study, perception is not a purely mental process restricted to individuals, but a phenomenon that is constituted through social participants' ongoing interaction. For instance, the complainee in Fragment (8) rejects with the complainant's perception that he has put a stop to the job of peeling fruit. In sum, in the course of the complaining activity, social participants display their perceptions, propose particular sociocultural norms, and claim certain conduct to be wrong. In response, other participants affirm or contest these propositions. The complaining activity is therefore a dynamic area in which participants interactively negotiate their perceptions, sociocultural norms, and wrongness of conduct through actual language use.

4.2.4. After Responses—No Further Contesting

This section examines what happens after the complainees respond to direct complaints. After complainees' responses, the complaining activity can be ended without further argument, or can be expanded, depending on what the original complainants do. Let me first present a context in which original complainants avoid further argument. They do so by not responding to the complainees' responses, or by downgrading their initial position after the responses. When they do not respond, the complainees' responses often end up doing the work of closing the complaint sequence. Fragments (4), and (6) in the preceding section are such cases. They are reproduced as Fragments (11) and (12) in the following.

(11) [Pizza Gathering]

1   Yun: *안녕하세요 이발 또 하셨네요,=

               *annyengha-sey-yo. ipal tto ha-sy-ess-ney-yo,=

               *: ((bow at Min))

               "How are you? ((/literally, 'Are you well?')) ((You)) got a haircut again,"=

2   Min: =안녕 못 하다.

             =annyeng <u>mos</u> ha-ta.
             "((I)) can <u>not</u> be well."

3   Yun: 왜요:.

             way-yo:.
             "Why:.."

4   Min: 니가 늦게 와가지구.=

             ni-ka nuckey w-akacikwu.=
             "Because you came late."

5   Yun: =.h 죄송합니다:. haha .h *↑죄송[합니다↑] .h
                                   *: ((take a deep bow))

             =.h coysongha-pnita:. haha .h *↑COYSONG[ha-pnita↑] .h
             =".h ((I)) am sorry:. haha .h ↑((I)) am SORRY↑ .h"

6   Suh: [°여기 앉아라.°]

                                           [°yeki anc-ala.°]
                                           "((to Yun)) °Sit down here.°"

7 → {(1.0)/ ((Yun sits down next to Suh))
8 → ((Suh asks Yun if her meeting ended late))

(12) [Pizza Gathering]

((Won working on Lego construction, and everybody else gathered at table))

1   Min: 아으 야 자 이 오바하지 말구 빨리 피자 먹어:.

             au ya ca i opa-ha-ci mal-kwu ppalli phica mek-e:.
             "Au hey now, don't do opa ((/'go overboard')), but come and eat the pizza already:!"

2   Won: °이게 더 재밌어요:.°

             °i-key te caymiss-eyo:.°
             "°This is more fu:n!°"

3 → (17.0)/ ((Won keeps working on Lego construction and the others start eating))}
4 → ((Suh asks another guest a question about one of her acquaintances))

88   *Chapter 4*

In Fragment (11), the complaint sequence is closed after Yun's apology since the complainant does not respond to it and another participant subsequently opens a new sequence (line 8). This is similar to Robinson's finding (2004) based on English data that people rarely respond to sorry-based apologies when these apologies are in the second pair part position. In Fragment (12), the response to the complaint is account-giving ("°This is more fu:n!°"), which is different from an apology. The complaint sequence still ends up being closed after the account-giving response when the complainant, Min, does not respond to it and the participants open a new sequence with a new topic after a long silence. Whereas both of the complaint sequences in Fragments (11) and (12) are closed by the complainees' second pair parts, the nonresponses to them by the complainant (Min in both cases) seem to operate differently. First, in Fragments (11), in which the complainee accepts the inadequacy of her behavior, the complainant's nonresponse implies that he accepts the complainees' apology. The complaint response in Fragment (12) is account-giving, and it does not acknowledge the problematic feature of the complained-about action. With this account, the complainee, Won, not only attempts to justify his action but also refuses to comply with the request conveyed through the preceding complaint. This response has thus developed the contesting environment. However, the complainant, Min, does not contest Won's non-cooperative response. Instead, he produces a silence and starts to eat without Won. A prior study interprets a silence at third position after a counter-assertion in argument sequences as an implicit backdown attributable to the first speaker (Coulter 1990). Min's silence in this fragment also shows that he is not further contesting or pursuing argument, although he might still consider the target conduct to be inappropriate.

Another way of avoiding further argument after a complainee's contesting response is producing a brief remark, which is a downgrade from the original complaining position. We can see an instance in Fragment (13), which is a conversation among three family members, a wife, her husband, and his younger sister. They are having spaghetti for lunch, and the husband complains about the state of spaghetti noodles in line 1.

(13) [Family Lunch] (Slightly Simplified)

1   Hus: °아유° .h 덜 익었잖아. (이거).

                °*aywu*° .h *tel ik-ess-canh-a. (i -ke).*

                "°*Aywu*° ((they)) are undercooked, you know! (These noodles)."

2   Wife: *↑괜[찮은데:,↑]   *: ((looks at Sister-in-law))

                *↑*kwayn*[*chanh-untey:,*↑]

Organization of Complaining Activity   89

                     "↑((They)) are <u>O</u>K ((to me)), tho:ugh↑"

3   Sis: [원래 이렇]게 먹는 건데 오빠.=

                    [*wenlay ileh*]*key mek-nun ke-ntey oppa,*=

                    "This is the way ((we)) are supposed to eat them, Brother,"=

4   Wife: =괜찮은데,

                    =*kwaynchanh-untey,*

                    "((They)) are okay, you know,"

5   {(1.5)/ ((Wife eats and Sis looks at Hus))}

6   Hus: [°(내가--)°]

                    [°*(nay-ka--)*°]

                    "°(I--)°"

7   Sis: [라면]도 원래 덜 익혀 먹잖아:.

                    [*lamyen*]*-to wenlay tel ikhy-e mek-cy-ahn-a:.*

                    "((We)) are supposed to eat <u>r</u>amen noodles undercooked, too, you kno:w."

8   (.)

9 → Hus: **그러니?**

                    kule-ni?

                    "Is that so?"

10   {(1.5)/ ((Participants eating))}

11   Wife: [으:음,]

                    [*u:um,*]

                    "Yea:h,"

12   Sis: [원래] 퍼지면 맛이 이상해[:.

                    [*wenlay*] *pheci -myen mas i isanghay*[:.

                    "If ((they)) are overcooked and soggy, ((they)) taste we:ird."

13   Wife: [음:. 이: 이게 딱 좋아.

                                      [*u:m. i: ikey ttak coh-a.*

                                      "Ye:s. Thi:s this is just right."

14 (0.8)
15 → Hus: °그래?°
             °*kulay?*°
             "°It is?°"
16 (0.5)
17 Wife: °음.°
             °*um.*°
             "°Yes.°"
18 {(10.0)/ ((Participants eating))}
19 ((Wife talks about repairing their car))

The wife's response in line 2 ("↑((They)) are O̱K ((to me)), tho:ugh↑") disagrees with the state of the noodles the husband complains about. While issuing this disagreeing response, she seeks support from her sister-in-law through her eye-gaze. The sister instantly, even before the wife finishes her turn, provides a supportive claim in line 3 ("This is the way ((we)) are supposed to eat them, Brother,") and joins in disagreeing with the husband. Whereas the wife has expressed what she personally thinks about the specific noodles that they are currently eating, the sister provides a claim that it is a standard way of cooking spaghetti noodles ("This is the way ((we)) are supposed to eat them, Brother,"). In this way, the sister not only agrees with the wife, but further heightens the level of disagreement with the husband's complaint. Upon the sister's supportive claim, the wife makes an immediate utterance, without pause, repeating what she said in her preceding complaint response (line 4).

After their collaborative disagreeing action, the sister checks, through her eye-gaze in line 5, if the husband is going to modify his original position. The husband, however, does not immediately respond to the sister and wife's disagreements (silence in line 5), which makes the sister provide another ground for her claim that undercooked noodles taste better (line 7). After a bit of pause, he produces a question with a pro-verb, *kule-ni?* ("Is that so?"), in line 9, which takes the place of the proposition in the sister's preceding utterance ("((We)) are supposed to eat ramen noodles undercooked, too, you know."). This utterance displays that the speaker takes the other participant's account as news (Oh 2002, 322), as repeats, partial repeats, or pro-repeats (such as "it is?"), and "really?" in English (all with or without a preceding "oh") serve as "newsmarks" (Heritage 1984b, citing Jefferson 1981). The husband's utterance, *kule-ni?*, marks his sister's remark as news, and thus provides her a chance to talk more about it. Although this newsmark is directed to the sister, the wife, who rejected the husband's complaint in the first place and asked for the sister's support, responds in line 11 with a confirmation, and displays her position as the same as the sister's. Such a confirmation to a newsmark can preempt the expansion of talking about the topic (Schegloff 2007, 157) and it can be followed by an assessment which is generally terminal or topic curtailing (Heritage 1984b, 340, citing Jefferson 1981, 62–66). However, in an overlap with the wife, the sister accepts the husband's invitation to talk further and gives another account that overcooked noodles are bad for texture and taste (line 12). The wife joins the sister in elaborating their claim, through her absolute agreement in line 13.

After the sister and the wife's collaborative telling about a standard way of cooking noodles, a relevant response would be the husband's acceptance. However, the husband does not produce one, but instead, issues the same newsmark again in line 15 after a pause, this time with soft voice quality. The other party does not make further significant attempt to solicit an acceptance from him, either: The sister does not respond at all, and the wife simply confirms his newsmark, also with soft voice quality (line 17). The use of soft voice quality displays the two parties' orientation to the closure of the complaint sequences, and the sequences are indeed closed after the wife's confirmation. Although the husband does not show a sign of actually agreeing with the other party's cooking standard, his use of the newsmark exhibits that he downgrades from his original complaining position. In his complaint, he made clear that he definitely regarded the noodles as improperly undercooked. However, he later takes it as news, through the newsmark, that undercooked noodles are better. That is, he treats it as new information which he did not know about. He does not produce a token of accepting that information, but he does not explicitly reject it or disagree, either. He thus takes a neutral position about the other participants' claim, which is a downgrade from his original explicit complaint. This downgraded newsmark then leads to the closure of the expanded complaint sequences without further argument.

4.2.5. After Responses—Further Contesting

The complainants often choose to contest the complainees' responses when they reject the complaints. Fragment (14) below shows an example. It is an extended version of Fragment (7) in this chapter (4.2.2) in which Jo complains toward his roommate Hoy because Hoy watched a TV show without him. As discussed earlier, Hoy responds with a challenge question and thereby rejects the complaint (line 3).

(14) [Roommate Talk] (Slightly simplified)

1 Jo: °아으: (혼자) 보냐 같이 보°·°°(기로 해놓고.)°°

    °au: (honca) po-nya kathi po°-°°(ki-lo hay-noh-ko.)°°

    "°*Au:* how could ((you)) watch it (without me)? After ((we)) decided° °°to watch it together.°°"

2 {(1.5)/ ((Jo looks at Hoy))}

3 Hoy: 하루종일 뭐 할까.

    halwucongil mwe ha-l-kka.

    "What would ((I)) do all day long then?"

4 (0.8)

5 → Jo: **한 게임.**

    han keyim.

    "A ((computer)) game."

6 (0.3)

7 Hoy: 어:? °(할 일)° <u>되</u>지게 없다. ((laug[h))

    e:? °(ha-l il)° <u>toy</u>cikey eps-ta. ((laug[h))

    "Hu:h? It would be a <u>rid</u>iculous thing °(to do)°. ((laugh))"

8 Jo: [나 클라스에:(h),

                                   [*na khulasu-ey:(h),*

9   .h컴퓨터 랩에 있었거든요. 예:?

    .h khemphywuthe layp-ey iss-ess-ketun-yo. yey:?

    "At my cla:ss(h), .h I was in the computer lab, you know?"

10 (0.5)

11 ((Jo tells that he played computer game during his class))

Hoy's response to Jo's complaint, which is a challenge question, conveys an assertion that there is nothing else to do while he stays home all day long, and implies that there would not be an answer which Jo could provide. (See 3.2.2 for discussions on how interrogatives with questions words do challenging and complaining instead of asking real questions.) However, Jo treats it as a real question and provides an answer ("A ((computer)) game." in line 5) that Hoy could have played a computer game instead of watching the video show without him. Such a response, which conforms to the grammatical form of the question, denies the implication that the question is unanswerable and thereby rejects the challenge (Koshik 2017). Jo's response to the complainee's second pair part thus displays that he is upholding his original position that Hoy's target behavior is complainable. Hoy in turn issues a counter-argument that it would be a ridiculous thing to do (line 7) and thereby maintains his challenging stance toward Jo's complaint. Following this expansion after the base complaint-response sequence, Jo opens a new sequence (line 8), and thereupon the complaint sequences are closed down without a co-establishment of complainability.

Fragment (14) has shown an example in which the complainee contests the complaint and the complainant further contests against it. In some cases, complainants choose to further contest even when the complainees have not challenged the original complaints in their responses. Fragment (15) illustrates an example in which the complainees respond to the complaint with account-giving and the complainant rejects the accounts. It is taken from the conversation among five friends who are having dinner at Young and Jeong's place. In the immediately preceding context, the participants began to eat, and they keep eating without talking for a long time (10.5 seconds in line 1 and 7.5 seconds in line 3 in this fragment). Young, who was a liaison between the conversation participants and the researcher for the video-taping, complains about the participants' long silence and at the same time requests them to talk (line 4). Then, one of the participants Jeong provides an account as a response in line 5.

(15) [Dinner Talk among Five Friends]

1   (10.5)
2   Young: °음°
                °um°
                "°Uhm°"

3   (7.5)
4   Young: *말 좀 해:*   ((l [a u g h))]
                MAL COM HAY: ((l [a u g h))]   * *: ((laugh voice))
                "PLEASE TA:LK ((laugh))"

5   Jeong: [((chuckle)) *먹]는   중[에 뭐]*
                                [((chuckle)) *m]ek-nuncwu[ng-ey mwe]*
                                                             * *: ((smile voice))
                                "((chuckle)) What, ((we)) are in the middle of eating"

6   Young: [왜 일]부러
                                                        [WAY i]lpwule

```
7                말들을 안 하구 그래:. ((laugh)) .h

                 mal-tul-ul an ha-kwu kulay:. ((laugh)) .h
                 "WHY are ((you guys)) intentionally not saying anythi:ng?
                 ((laugh)) .h"

8    Hoon:       막: 말을 하다가두,

                 ma:k mal-ul ha-taka-twu,
                 "Even when we are talking a lo:t,"

9    Young:     응.

                 ung.
                 "Yes."

10   Hoon:      >이렇게< 딱 먹을 때는 ( . ) 조용히 있어.

                 >ilehkey< ttak mek-ul ttay-nun ( . ) coyonghi °iss -e.°
                 "when we eat >like this< ( . ) we just °stay quiet°."

11   (0.8)

12→ Young:      °아니° 너 안 그러잖아[:

                 °ani° ne an kule-c-anh-a[:
                 "°No° you don't do that, you kno:w"

13   (Joo/Jeong):                   [((lau[gh))
14   Suk:                                [((chuckle))
15   (2.2)
16   Young:     °mm° 맛있다.

                 °mm° masiss-ta.
                 "°Mm° ((It)) is delicious."
```

Jeong's response in line 5 is an account that they are not talking because they are in the middle of eating. Young does not reject or challenge Jeong's second pair part but upgrades the first pair part complaint by characterizing the absence of talk as an "intentional" act in lines 6 and 7 ("WHY are ((you guys)) intentionally not saying anythi:ng?"). In this way, she renews her complaining action and expands the complaining activity. Another complainee Hoon also responds to this upgraded complaint with a similar account (lines 8 and 10) as Jeong's previous one. The complainant reacts this time with a rejection of that account in line 12. The complainees avoid further argument by producing laugh tokens after that (lines 13 and 14), and thereupon the complaint sequences are closed.

Post-expansions (Schegloff 2007) in which the complainants and the complainees further confront each other after a base complaint-response pair do not always occur through the complainants' challenge to the complainees' responses or reworkings of their original complaints. As Schegloff (2007) notes, the structuring of post-expansions can become increasingly less determinate because they are hardly disciplined or constrained by the base first pair part or second pair part. Fragment (16) in the following presents another example of an indefinite number of ways in which the participants develop their confronting positions in post-expansions. It is an extended version of Fragment (9) in 4.2.2, in which Min complains that Won treated him with arrogance when he asked for some help. In response, Won counter-complains that it was Min who brought too many materials to handle at a time (lines 6 and 7).

(16) [Pizza Gathering] (Slightly Simplified)

1   Yun: 사층에 계속 계셨어요?

            sa-chung-ey kyeysok kyeysy-ess-eyo?
            "Did ((you)) stay on the fourth floor for a long time?"

2   (1.0)

3   Min: 아니 뭐 찍는 거 부탁하느라구

            ani mwe ccik-nun ke pwuthakha-nulakwu
            "Well uh because ((I)) needed to ask ((Won)) a favor, some help with measuring"

4   *아이구:[: 저 인간 유]세하는 거 때문에 내가 아주,

            aikwu:[: ce inkan ywu]seyha-nun ke ttaymwuney nay-ka acwu,
            * ((Min's eye-gaze changing from Yun to Won. Also, moving his head forward a little while producing *aikwu::*, as if he were striking Won with his head.))

            "*Aikwu::* because that human being ((/a despicable expression of 'person')) was showing so much arrogance, I was so like"

5   Won: [↑아유::↑]

                      [↑ *a y w u :: ↑*]
                      "↑*Aywu::*↑"

6   Won: >무슨< 유세를 해요↓ 한꺼번에 저렇게

7   다 갖구와가지구↓

         >mwusun< ywusey-lul hay-yo↓ hankkepeney celehkey
         ta kackwuw-akacikwu↓ hu

         "What arrogance did ((I)) sho↓w? ((You)) brought all the materials at once like tha↓t hu"

8   Suh: 찍는거 부탁해?

         ccik-nun ke pwuthakhay?
         "Asking a favor of measuring?"

((Many lines omitted: Won provides an explanation on for what Min asked for his help))

9→ Won: 그래서 민이 형이 뭐 하나 잘 안 만들어지고

10   있었 [거든요¿]

         kulayse Mini hyeng-i mwe hana cal an mantul-e ci -ko
         iss-ess[-ketun-yo¿]

         "And so Brother Mini was having one thing that was not working out well, you know¿"

11 Yun: [그래가지구] (0.5) 유세를 엄청 [했어]요?

         [(kulay)-kacikwu] (0.5) ywusey-lul emcheng [hay-ss-e]yo?=
         "((toward Min)) Because of (that) (0.5) did ((Won)) show so much arrogance ((to you))?"=

12 Min: [°↓에:↓°]

                                                     [°↓ey:↓°]
                                                     "°↓u:h↓°"

13→ Won: =유세 하나두 안 했어요 무슨 유세야↓

         =YWUSEY HANA-TWU AN HAY-SS-EYO mwusun ywusey-ya↓
         ="((I)) DID NOT SHOW ANY ARROGANCE AT ALL. What arrogance are ((you)) talking abo↓ut?"

14 Min: 하나도 안 하기는: 인간[아↓.]

         hana-to an ha-ki-nu:n. inkan[-a↓.]
         "No arrogance at all? You je↓rk."

Organization of Complaining Activity 97

15→Won: [아]니 찍어준다고: *했드니만*

           [AN]I CCIKEcwu-ntako: *hay-ss-tuni-man*

                                   * *: ((laugh voice))

16→   *여덟 갠가 [아홉] 열 갠가* ha .h

        yetelp kay-nka [ahop] yel kay-nka ha .h

        * *: ((laugh voice))

        "I MEAN WHEN I SAID(h) I WOULD DO THE MEASUring *work* ((for him)), ((he brought)) *eight, or nine, or was it ten* ha .h"

17 Yun: [어흐]

        [ehu]

        "Whew"

18→Won: >(그[걸 꼭<]

        >(ku-[ke-l) kkok<]

        ">(all of those), necessarily<"

19 Min: [무슨] 여덟 개[야:: 여섯 개지 : .]

        [mwusun] yetelp kay[-ya : : yeses kay-ci : .]

        "What eight thi::ngs. It was si:x."

20→Won: [한꺼번에 (다 못 찍죠 그)걸:]

        [hankkepeney (ta mos ccik-cy-o ku)-ke:-l]

        "((We)) can't measure all of them at once, you know. Those thi:ngs"

21 {(1.0)/ ((Yun and Suh go to kitchen))}

22→Won: 나눠서는 찍어두:.

        nanw-ese-nun ccik-etwu:.

        "Although ((we)) can measure ((them)) if ((we)) divi:de ((them))."

23 {(0.6)/ ((Child's laugh sound from the room))}

24 Won: [어]

        [e]

        "Oh"

25 Suh: [냉]장고에 없는데 윤아,

              [*nay*]*ngcangko-ey eps-nuntey Yun-a,*
              "It's not in the fridge, Yun"

26 {(6.5)/ ((Child's laugh sound from the room))}

27 Won: 저 우는 거 아냐?

              ce wu-nun ke any-a?
              "Isn't that a crying sound?"

After Won's counter-complaint, another participant, Suh, displays his trouble understanding Won's utterance, and requests more information ("Asking a favor of measuring?" in line 8). As an answer, Won explains what kind of help Min needed from him, and as he is about to finish his explanation (lines 9 and 10), Yun interrupts and displays her interpretation of what happened ("Because of (that) (0.5) did ((Won)) show so much arrogance ((to you))?" in line 11). However, her interpretation is not neutral, but takes an affiliative stance with Min's version which was delivered through his original complaint. She directs this utterance toward Min and seeks confirmation of her understanding from him. However, Won, instead of Min, takes an immediate turn and expresses a strong disagreement marked with loudness in line 13 ("((I)) DID NOT SHOW ANY ARROGANCE AT ALL."). Then, he issues a challenge in the form of a RPQ with *mwusun* ("what") ("What arrogance are ((you)) talking abo:ut?"). This is a response to Yun's candidate understanding, and at the same time it is a challenge to Min's original complaint, toward which Yun has been empathetic. Min responds with a counter-challenge that shows his position upholding his initial complaint (line 14). With the use of the contrastive marker *-ki-nun* ("on the contrary"), the despicable expression of "person" *inkan*, and the later upward intonation which carries a protesting tone, he clearly indicates that he is disagreeing with and challenging Won's claim that he did not show any arrogance at all.

Won rejects this challenge from Min again in his multiple turns from line 15 to 22: He first mentions his initial willingness to help ("I MEAN WHEN I SAID(h) I WOULD DO THE MEASUring work ((for him))" in line 15), and then presents specific numbers of the materials which Min brought for help ("((he brought)) eight, or nine, or was it ten" in line 16). By doing so, he claims that he was willing to help but the amount of work was too much for him to handle at once. Min interrupts him and disagrees with the numbers that were just specified ("What eight thi::ngs. It was si:x." in line 19). Whereas Won specified the numbers from eight to ten, Min only mentions the lowest number, eight, and then disagrees with it by claiming that he brought six. In doing so, he tries to describe the amount of work to have been as little as possible. However, Won does not respond to Min's repair of the number, but continues his argument ("((We)) can't measure all of them at once, you know. Those thi:ngs" in line 20) in an overlap with Min's disagreement. After their overlapping utterances end at the same time, silence follows, and Won produces an additional remark ("Although ((we)) can measure ((them)) if ((we)) divi:de ((them))."), through which he sustains his position. Min does not respond any more and Won does not further his argument, either. Thereupon, the complaining activity between Min and Won, which has been extensively expanded after the base complaint-response sequence, is closed without either party's explicit concession.

4.2.6. After Responses—Summary

I have demonstrated the ways in which the original complainants avoid confrontation or sustain their stances after the complainees' second pair parts. In cases where the complainees acknowledge the complainability in their responses, the complainants tend to implicitly accept the responses by not responding to them, and the complaint sequences are closed after the second pair parts, as in Fragment (11). The complaint sequences can also be closed after the second pair parts when the complainees reject the complaints, as in Fragment (12). In these cases, the complainants' nonresponse shows that they are simply avoiding further confrontation. I have also shown an instance in which the complainant downgrades from the original complaint after the complainee's challenging response, as in Fragment (13). However, in many cases where the complainees' responses reject the complaints, the complainants further contest the complainees' second pair parts and expand the complaint sequences, as in Fragments (14) and (16). In other cases, complainants choose to further contest even when the complainees have not challenged the original complaints in their responses, as in Fragment (15). In the expansions of complaint sequences after the second pair parts, the two parties often sustain their positions and thereby keep up the confrontation. Such expanded complaint sequences are likely to be closed without explicit agreement between the two parties, when either of them stops responding, as seen in Fragments (14)—(16).

4.3. SEQUENCING IN INDIRECT COMPLAINT ACTIVITY

Now we move to the cases of indirect complaints. Their sequences are examined in this section based on the degree of affiliative stances displayed in the responses to the complaints. Recipients of indirect complaints have less interactional burden than those who must respond to direct complaints produced face to face. However, in responding to indirect complaints, the recipients unavoidably create a particular relational atmosphere with the complainants as well. When complainants have just shared their negative evaluations of target events and expressed their affective stances toward them through indirect complaints, the recipients' remarks respond not only to the complainants' evaluations, but also to their affective stances. The responses may be affiliative, or they may not be. Affiliation is explained as "the affective level of cooperation" (Stivers et al. 2011, 21), meaning that affiliative responses provide cooperation to the first speakers by showing the same evaluative stance and empathy. Affiliative responses to indirect complaints are thus prosocial actions through which the respondents support the complainants at the affective level. (They explain another form of interactional cooperation at the structural level, alignment, which I will discuss related to Fragment (20) later in this section.)

This section examines affiliative, neutral, or somewhat disaffiliative responses to indirect complaints. Explicitly disaffiliative ones are not a primary focus of this book because the majority of the responses in my data are affiliative to different degrees, or are at least neutral. Also, disaffiliative responses are complex actions, such as disagreements, involving extensions and expansions of the ongoing activities with a variety of intricate practices, which takes the investigation beyond the scope of this book.

4.3.1. Affiliating Responses to Indirect Complaints

The following fragment presents an example posted anonymously on an online community, in which registered members interact based on a variety of topics, and illustrates how respondents affiliate through indirect complaints.

(17) [Web Community Post 1, www.todayhumor.co.kr]

Original post:
아이고 힘들다... 외롭다. 나만 그런게 아니겠지.
aiko himtul-ta . . . oylop-ta. na-man kulen-key ani-keyss-ci.
"*Aiko* ((it)) is hard . . . ((I)) am lonely. I may not be the only one like that, right?"

Response 1:
ㅠㅠ

Response 2:
다들 그럴거에요.

ta-tul kulel-ke-ey-yo

"Everyone will be like that"

Response 3:

나도요... 외롭네요 ㅜㅜㅜㅜㅜㅜ

na-to-yo ... oylop-ney-yo ㅜㅜㅜㅜㅜㅜ

"Me, too ... ((I)) am lonely. ㅜㅜㅜㅜㅜㅜ?"

Response 4:

아이고 힘들다 + 외롭다 + 우울하다 ㅠㅠ

aiko himtul-ta + oylop-ta + wuwulha-ta ㅠㅠ

"*Aiko* ((it)) is hard + ((I)) am lonely + ((I)) am depressed ㅠㅠ"

The original post is a complaint about a hardship and loneliness which the posting member is experiencing. Although it is an anonymous post, which does not specify what sort of hardship he or she is going through, other members express their empathic stances toward it: Respondent 1 by using an emoticon, ㅠ symbolizing an eye shedding tears, twice, Respondent 2 by saying that "everyone" shares similar hardship and loneliness and thereupon implying that they will understand the complainant's emotional state, and Respondents 3 and 4 by offering sympathy based on their own similar feelings.

The following is another example of affiliative responses to a more specific indirect complaint posted anonymously on another web community whose members are mostly married women and in which they interact regarding various topics. After the original poster complains about her own forgetfulness of getting the coffee that she ordered and paid for, a series of responses express affiliative stances.

(18) [Web Community Post 2, www.missyusa.com]

Original post:

저 커피 오더해놓고 그냥 왔어요 내가 미쳤나 치매가 오려나

커피 오더를 해놓곤 완전히 잊어버리고 그냥 나왔어요 ㅠㅠㅠㅠㅠㅠ

ce khephi otehay-noh-ko kuynyang wa-ss-eyo nay-ka michye-ss-na chimay-ka olye-na

khephi otehay-noh-ko-n wancenhi icepeli-ko kunyang nawa-ss-eyo ㅠㅠㅠㅠ ㅠㅠ

"I ordered coffee and then I came without it. Am I crazy. Am ((I)) having dementia. After ordering coffee, ((I)) completely forgot ((about it)) and got out without it ㅠㅠㅠㅠㅠㅠㅠ"

Response 1:

저도 예전에 드라이브 뜨루에서 커피랑 아침 메뉴 주문해 놓고, 아침 메뉴만 싹 받아서 휙 차 몰고 그냥 온 적 있어요. 원래 주 목적은 커피였었는데...

ce-to yeycen-ey tulaipu ttulwu-eyse khephi-lang achim meynywu cwumwun-hay noh-ko, achim meynywu-man ssak pat-ase hwik cha mol-ko kunyang o-n cek iss-eyo. wenlay cwu mokcek-un khephi-y-ess-ess-nuntey. . .

"I also have an experience of ordering coffee and breakfast at drive-through, getting the breakfast only, and then driving away without coffee. My main goal was originally to get coffee. . ."

Response 2:

그렇게 놓고 가는 커피가 스벅 매장당 하루 평균 100잔이라더군요. 흔한 일이니까 너무 자책하지 마세요

kulekkey noh-ko ka-nun khephi-ka supek maycang-tang halwu phyengkywun 100 can-i-la-te-kwun-yo. hunha-n il-i-nikka nemwu cachaykha-ci ma-sey-yo

"((They)) say the average number of coffees which are not taken like that is 100 per day at each Starbucks location. Since it happens so frequently, don't blame yourself too much."

Response 3:

Drive thru로 주문하고 돈 내고 그냥 휑 달려 출근한 적도 여러번 ㅠㅠ

Drive thru-lo cwumwunha-ko ton nay-ko kunyang hweyng tally-e chwul-kunha-n cek-to yele-pen ㅠㅠ

"((I've)) made an order at drive-thru, made the payment, and then just driven away without ((getting my order)) to get to work several times ㅠㅠ"

Respondents 1 and 3 display empathetic stances by sharing their own similar or even worse experiences and Respondent 2 comforts the original poster by providing a statistical result showing that many people make the same mistakes. These responses as well as the ones in Fragment (17) are all commiserating, which Boxer (1993a) finds to be a common action done through indirect complaint exchanges. She explains commiserating in indirect complaints to be a positive social function because it establishes rapport and a sense of solidarity between participants by communicating a shared view.

Participants in oral conversation frequently respond to indirect complaints with affiliative stances as well. Fragment (19) presents an example. It is taken from a conversation among three male friends who are studying abroad as graduate students at an American university. In the immediately preceding context, Hyun has complained that his new laptop got broken and he tried many different ways to have it fixed through the laptop company, HP, but none of them worked. In line 1 in the following, Hyun initiates another sequence of complaining about the company's suggestions not being helpful.

(19) [Computer Talk] (Slightly simplified)

1   Hyun: 여기 아-- 뭐야 <HP에서 authorize한:,>

                 yeki a-- mwe-ya <HP-eyse authorize ha:-n,>
                 "Here uhm-- what is it <HP-authori:zed,>"

2   Koo: °음[:°

                 °u [:m°
                 "°Uh hu:h°"

3   Hyun: [이런: 고치는 곳이 있대요.

                 [*ile:n kochi-nun kos-i iss-tay-yo.*
                 "they say that there is a repair place like tha:t ((authorized by HP))."

4   Koo: 아:[:

                 a : [:
                 "O::h"

5   Hyun: [*거기가* h .h [best] buy야:. ((l[a u g] h))=

                 [**keki-ka* h .h [best] buy-ya:. ((l[a u g] h))=*
                 * *: ((laugh voice))
                 "That place is h .h Best Bu:y. ((laugh))"

6 → Koo: [(be)--]   [얘네 기--]

                 [*(be)--*]   [*yay-ney ki--*]
                 "Be--"   "These guys' ski--"

7   Hyun: =best bu(h)y   ((l[a u g h)) .HH]=

8 → Koo: [기술 없어 별루::: 아유 씨 간--]

                 [*kiswul eps-e pyellwu::: aywu ssi kan--*]
                 "((They)) do not have skill, not mu:::ch *aywu ssi* simp--"

9	Hyun:	=*개넬 뭘 믿구 가서 거기서 그걸*= * *: ((laugh voice))

=*KYAY-NEY-L MWE-L MIT-KWU ka-se keki-se ku-ke-l*=
"HOW CAN ((I)) TRUST THEM and take it there"

10→	Koo:	=간단한 거만 [고치지:] 걔네: (0.5) 뭐 다이아그노스=

=*kantanhan ke-man* [*kochi-ci:*] *kyay-ney:* (0.5) *mwe diagnos*=
"((They)) fix only simple thi:ngs, those guy:s. (0.5) Uh for diagnosis"

11	Hyun:	[그 럼 :]

                    [*kule:m*]
                    "Of cou:rse"

12→	Koo:	=한다구 육[십 불] 그-- 팔십 [불]

=*ha-ntakwu ywuk*[*sip pwul*] *ku-- phalsip* [*pwul*]
"((they charge)) sixty dollars uh-- eighty dollars"

13	Hyun:	[그럼:] [육십]오 불.

           [*kule:m*]   [*ywuksi*]*p-o pwul.*
           "Of cou:rse"   "Sixty five dollars."

14→	Koo:	어:. 그냥 받아버리는 거야,

e:. kunyang pat-apeli-nun ke-ya,
"Ye:s. ((They)) just take the money ((without even fixing it))."

In lines 1 and 3, Hyun says that the computer company recommended a repair place authorized by them. Koo cooperates by facilitating Hyun's telling through a continuer (Schegloff 1982) in line 2 (°*u:m*°, "°Uh hu:h°"), which acknowledges that Hyun's turn will continue. Koo also indicates through a change-of-state token (Heritage 1984a) in line 4 (*a:*, "O::h") that he is finding the information on the existence of a repair place to be new to him. Slightly overlapping with Koo's change-of-state token, Hyun reveals the complete information on the authorized repair place in line 5 by saying it is Best Buy, an electronics retailer. The way he delivers this information is quite dramatic: He uses laughing voice at the beginning of the sentence ("That place is"), delays the next part of the announcement through an out-breath and an in-breath ("h .h"), then utters the name of the place, and puts an emphasis through vowel lengthening at the sentence ending, and adds laughter after the utterance. He mentions the name of the place once again and extends the laughter in line 7. Laughter plays many different roles in complaining activities depending on its contexts (e.g., Clift 2012, 2016; Holt 2012; Jefferson 1984). As an example, laughter is often employed in a complaint about a third party (Clift 2012), and its function is to exhibit that "although there is this trouble, it is not getting the better of him; he is managing; he is in good spirits and in a position to take the trouble lightly" (Jefferson 1984, 351). Hyun's utterance in lines 5 and 7 is such a case: He reports the upshot of the laptop company's recommendation in a dramatic way with extended laughter, by which he delivers a message that their recommendation is laughably unhelpful, and thus complainable, but that he is taking the problem lightly.

Koo initiates his response in line 6 as soon as Hyun reveals the information on the repair place. He withdraws his response when Hyun produces his first laughter, but delivers his response from line 8, in an overlap with Hyun's second laughter. Koo's response is a strong complaint about the company's recommendation: He asserts that the workers at the recommended retailer do not have much skill, and in so doing, he employs an elongated later upward intonation (*pyellwu:::*) and response cries (*aywu ssi*) both of which are recurrently used resources for complaining (see 3.1 and 3.3). In this way, Koo positions himself as a co-complainant, which is highly affiliative with the original complainer's stance. Based on Koo's affiliative response in line 8, Hyun issues another complaint in line 9 ("How can ((I)) trust them and take it there") with a loud voice quality (*KYAY-NEY-L MWE-L MIT-KWU* "HOW CAN ((I)) TRUST THEM") and a stress on the question word (*MWE-L*) of the question conveying the reversed polarity assertion ("I can't trust them at all and so can't take it there"). Koo continues his own co-complaint in lines 10 and 12 by asserting that they fix only simple things and charge an expensive fee for a diagnosis alone. He utters his estimations of the diagnostic fee ("sixty dollars" and "eighty dollars") and Hyun provides a correct amount in line 13 ("sixty five dollars"). Koo acknowledges it (*e:.*) and then completes his complaint utterance in line 14.

Koo's response in this fragment turns one party's complaining action into a complaining activity in which both parties share the same view and stance. Koo's responsive complaint about the same complainable event elaborates on why the computer company's recommendation is ludicrous. Hyun provides a correction on the diagnostic fee in the middle of Koo's responsive complaining process, and Koo accepts it and then completes his action. The whole process shows that Koo's affiliative response creates an atmosphere in which the two parties collaboratively complain about the computer company and its recommended repair place's uselessness. The participants thus utilize the complaining activity to construct social solidarity by sharing the same evaluative and affective stance.

4.3.2. Avoiding Fully Affiliating in Responses to Indirect Complaints

While participants frequently respond to indirect complaints with affiliative responses, they sometimes take less affiliative or somewhat disaffiliative stances in their responses. In such responses, avoiding fully affiliating, laughter becomes a useful resource (Holt 2012). The following fragment shows an example in a phone conversation between two male friends. Moon, the caller tells Kang in line 1 that there is a reason for calling, and says in line 2 that he is very upset because of his car, which is a complaint.

(20) [Phone Conversation between Kang and Moon]

1 Moon: 다름이 아니구,

talum-i ani-kwu,

"((The reason for calling)) is none other than,"

2 Kang: 음.

um.

"Yeah."

3 Moon: ↑아:↑ 나 >지금< 차 때문에 속이 상해가지구:

↑*a:*↑ *na* >*cikum*< *cha ttaymey sok-i sanghay-kacikwu:*

"↑A:↑ >now< I am so upset because of ((my)) ca:r"

4 Kang: 음.

um.

"Yeah."

5 Moon: 그: (.) h ((clear throat)) 엔진:,

ku: (.) *h* ((clear throat)) *eynci:n,*

"U:h (.) h ((clear throat)) engi:ne,"

6 Kang: 음.

um.

"Yeah."

7 ((extensive amount of turns deleted: Moon describing the car problem in detail and Kang responding with brief response tokens such as continuers or acknowledgement tokens (Gardner 2001)))

8 Moon: 차를 못 쓰겠다 차를

		cha-lul mos ssu-keyss-ta cha-lul
9		아:[이 짜증나
		a:[i ccacungna
		"((I)) can't use the car, this one. *A:i* ((I)) am so vexed"
10→	Kang:	[((c h u c k l [e))
11	Moon:	[알았어.=
		[al-ass-e.=
		"Okay, I see."
12	Kang:	=아이구. 중고차가 다 그렇지 어떡하냐:.=
		=aikwu. cwungko-cha-ka ta kuleh-ci ettekha-nya:.=
		"**Aikwu. Used cars are all like that. What can ((we)) do abou:t it.**"
13	Moon:	=아: 진짜 미치겠다. 그 뭐 칠천불 짜리구
		=a: cincca michi-keyss-ta. ku mwe chil-chen-pwul ccali-kwu
14		팔천불 짜리구 아무 소용 없구만.
		phal-chen-pwul ccali-kwu amwu soyong eps-kwuman.
		"*A:* really ((I)) am going crazy. Like, uh, whether ((it)) is 7,000 dollars or 8,000 dollars, ((it)) is no use at all."
15→	Kang:	**((chuckl[e))**
16	Moon:	[새 차 아닌 이상 인[제.
		[say cha ani-n isang in[cey.
		"unless ((it)) is a new car."
17	Kang:	[응:.
		[ung:.
		"Yea:h."

When Moon mentions that he is very upset about his car in line 3, Kang issues a simple continuer (*um.* "Yeah.") in line 4, indicating that Moon can continue telling him about it. Moon starts a telling sequence in line 5 and describes the problem of his car at great length in combination with expressing his upset state, which is omitted due to the limited space here. In the course of Moon's trouble-telling, Kang responds with brief response tokens such as continuers (e.g., *um.* in line 6) or acknowledgement tokens. Such responses from Kang play a role in facilitating the progress of the trouble-telling, another form of interactional cooperation at the structural level conceptualized as alignment by Stivers et al. (2011). Alignment is different from affilatiation in that it does not provide empathetic support to the teller while affiliation does. It only supports the teller in progressing the complaint narrative. Moon concludes his action of trouble-telling in lines 8 and 9, with another complaint utterance ("((I)) can't use the car, this one. *A:i* I am so vexed"). In response, Kang chuckles without explicitly affiliating or disaffiliating with Moon's affective stance in line 10.

Holt (2012) observes that complaint recipients use laughter when they move toward topic termination without developing the complaints further while responding to it. Moon shows an orientation to such a function of laughter in line 11 and indicates his intention to terminate the topic by saying "Okay, I see." Then, Kang produces an evaluative utterance about used cars in general, "*Aikwu.* Used cars are all like that. What can ((we)) do abou:t it." This general remark might have been made to move further toward terminating the topic. However, Moon responds to this non-affiliative general assessment with an additional complaint in lines 13 and 14 ("*A:* really ((I)) am going crazy. Like, uh, whether ((it)) is 7,000 dollars or 8,000 dollars, ((it)) is no use at all.") and thereby expands the sequence further. He might have done so to give another chance for Kang to affiliate with his affective stance, but Kang responds with another non-affiliative chuckle in line 15, which leads Moon to add another element to his prior complaining turn and recomplete it in line 16 ("unless ((it)) is a new car."), and yet Kang merely acknowledges it in line 17 ("Yea:h") without being explicitly empathetic. Kang displays his non-affiliative stance throughout the course of the complaining activity, and he utilizes chuckles as a central resource for maintaining such a stance.

Kang's responses including chuckles in the course of Moon's complaining are clearly non-affiliative and even disaffiliatve to some degree, but they are not explicitly disaffiliative, either. The degree of non-affiliation in laughter-embedded responses to indirect complaints differ, and the following fragments present examples with more affiliative responses than Kang's. Fragment (21) is a phone conversation between a mother who lives in Korea and her daughter who lives the United States. The mother complains about the snowy weather in Korea in line 1 and the daughter responds with a change-of-state token ("O:h") and a chuckle in line 2.

(21) [Phone Conversation between Mother and Daughter]

1   M: 눈 또 왔어:

            nwun tto wa-ss-e:

            "It snowed agai:n"

2 →D:		어: ((chuckle))
		e: ((chuckle))
		"O:h" ((chuckle))
3	M:	지겨워. ((c[huckle))]
		cikyew-e. ((c[huckle))]
		"((I)) am sick of it. ((chuckle))"
4 →D:		[((chuckle))] 웬일이야:=
		[((chuckle))] *weyn-il-i-ya:=*
		((chuckle)) "How co:me"=
5	M:	=반가운게 아니라,
		=*pankawu-n-key ani-la,*
		="It's not that ((I)) like it"
6 →D:		.h 그러게 말야. hu hu
		.h kulekey mal-ya. hu hu
		".h ((I)) know what ((you)) mean. hu hu"

After the daughter's response without explicit affiliation, the mother adds another complaint utterance in line 3 ("((I)) am sick of it.") with a chuckle possibly to make her complaint light. The daughter responds with another chuckle in line 4, followed by "How co:me" with a later upward intonation this time, which can be interpreted as an affiliative co-complaint. The mother extends her complaint again line 5 ("It's not that ((I)) like it"), and the daughter issues another affiliative response in line 6 ("I know what you mean.") along with a brief chuckle, which closes the complaint sequence.

In the following online posting, the respondents express their affiliative stances at various degrees, and a laugh symbol in one of the responses plays a role in displaying somewhat affiliative stance. The complaint in the online posting is from a mother about her four-year-old daughter's continuous demand of role-plays. (See Fragment (24) in 2.2.3 for the full text of the complaint.)

(22) [Web Community Post 3, www.missyusa.com]

Original post:
1   딸 키우시는 엄마분들... 이 짓을 언제까지 하나요? ㅠ

ttal khiwu-si-nun emma-pwun-tul. . . i-cis-ul encey-kkaci ha-na-yo? ㅠ

"Those of you moms who raise daughters. . . How long should ((I)) do this stupid thing? ㅠ"

2 4살 딸 키우고 있는데 하루종일 역할놀이에 빠져 있어요.

4-sal ttal khiwu-ko iss-nuntey halwu-congil yekhal-noli-ey ppacy-e iss-eyo.

"((I)) have a 4-year old daughter and ((I)) am dragged into role-play all day long."

3 인형놀이, 캠핑놀이, 공주놀이, 슈퍼놀이, 병원놀이,

inhyeng-noli, khaymphing-noli, kongcwu-noli, sywuphe-noli, pyengwen-noli,

"Doll-play, camping-play, princess-play, market-play, hospital-play,"

4 ((several lines deleted: detailing what she does to meet her daughter's demand))

5 아. . . 힘들어요 ㅠㅠ

a. . . himtul-eyo ㅠㅠ

"A. . . ((it)) is hard ㅠㅠ"

Response 1:

6살즈음되면서 조금씩 덜 찾아요. 그러다 8살 넘어가서는 뭐 필요할때만 찾구요. . . 아.. 진짜 그립네요. ㅎㅎ

6-sal-cuum-toy-myense cokum-ssik tel chac-ayo. kuleta 8-sal nemeka-se-nun mwe philyoha-l-ttay-man chac-kwu-yo. . . a.. cincca kulip-ney-yo. ㅎㅎ

"((They)) demand less when they become about 6 years old. After that, ((they)) look for ((us)) only when ((they)) need something. . . A.. ((I)) really miss ((the time)). ㅎㅎ"

Response 2:

에구 힘드시죠? 근데 전 막 상상이 되면서 너무 이쁠거 같아요. 약간 부럽다고 할까요?? 지금은 말도 잘 안하고 그런때가 있었나? 제 기억에만 있는거 같아요.

eykwu himtu-si-cy-o? kuntey ce-n mak sangsang-i toy-myense nemwu ippul-ke kath-ayo. yakkan pwulep-ta-ko ha-l-kka-yo?? cikum-un mal-to cal an ha-ko kule-n ttay-ka iss-ess-na? cey kiek-ey-man iss-nun-ke kath-ayo.

"*Eykwu* ((it)) is hard, right? But I can imagine ((the scenes)) and I think ((she)) must be adorable. ((I)) can say ((I)) am a bit envious?? ((My kid)) doesn't talk ((to me)) much now and ((I)) am wondering whether ((I)) actually had that time ((with my kid)). I think ((it)) exists only in my memory."

Response 3:

저도요... 저는 3살 딸이 저보고 자꾸 언니래요... 자기는 애기한다고... 아놔 미치겠음... ㅠㅠ

ce-to-yo... ce-nun 3-sal ttal-i ce-poko cakkwu enni-lay-yo... caki-nun ayki ha-nta-ko... a-nwa michi-keyss-um... ㅠㅠ

"Me, too... As for me, my 3-year-old daughter keeps calling me Sister... She says she plays a baby. Oh my, ((I)) am going crazy... ㅠㅠ"

Of the four responses, Respondent 3 shows the most affiliative stance with the original posting by using the same kind of complaint about her own daughter's similar demand. Respondent 2 shows a highly affiliative stance at the beginning ("*Eykwu* ((it)) is hard, right?") but shifts the focus from the complainable aspect to an adorable aspect of the same behavior by the child ("But I can imagine ((the scenes)) and I think ((she)) must be adorable."). Then, she characterizes the complainant's position as a bit enviable ("((I)) can say ((I)) am a bit envious??") and provides a ground for such a characterization from her own experience of passing through the stage a long time ago and missing it now. Response 1 is less affiliative than the other two. It does not directly address the complaining action performed in the original posting, but addresses only to the first line of the complaint which is composed in an interrogative format ("Those of you moms who raise daughters... How long should ((I)) do this stupid thing? ㅠ"). Although the interrogative sentence conveys a complaining assertion rather than asking a real question (see 3.2.2 for the use of such a sentence type for complaints), Respondent 1 treats it as a question and provides an answer ("((They)) demand less when they become about 6 years old. After that, ((they)) look for ((us)) only when ((they)) need something..."). Then, she expresses her stance as adoring young children's demand for play by releasing a response cry (*a..*) and saying she "really misses ((the time))." At the end, she adds ㅎㅎ, which is a laugh symbol utilizing a pair of a Korean consonant and its sound similar to laughter. The addition of the laugh symbol lightens the stance, which is not completely affiliative with the original complainant's frustrated state.

The varying degrees of affiliation in these responses show how each of the participants delicately handles the complex aspects of the target complainable and their identities. Collaboration can be a potentially problematic matter for complaint recipients because affiliating involves taking part in criticizing the actions of others that they may not wish to collaborate in (Holt 2012). In this fragment, the participants are all mothers and the complainable event is their children's behavior. While they commiserate with each other by sharing their difficulties, they should not want to be viewed as undesirable mothers lacking love and patience. Therefore, each response is supportive for the group identity as mothers in different ways: Response 3, the most affiliative one, focuses on commiserating and sympathizing about a difficulty of motherhood, and the other two provide a perspective of more experienced mothers at a later stage at which they look back the earlier time and remember it fondly. The experienced mothers imply that the complainant will feel the same way later, too, which is a way of embracing her as a loving mother even though she is complaining now. It is also a way of constructing their group identity as mothers and presenting desirable norms for loving mothers. The following chapter will discuss further how participants embody various kinds of social identities and memberships in complaining activities.

Chapter 5

Social Organization in Complaining Activity

This book has thus far explicated constructional and organizational features of turns and sequences in the complaining activity. This chapter shifts focus and explores how social organization such as social identities and relations is interactively negotiated and constituted through the complaining activity. Practices of constructing social identities and memberships have briefly been discussed in 4.3 based on indirect complaints, in which participants often establish solidarity and create group identities. The current chapter focuses on direct complaining, which is commonly considered to be a "face-threatening act" (Brown and Levinson 1987) and to be harmful to social relationships.

The relationship between social organization and talk-in-interaction has been investigated in CA and ethnomethodological research. Some of the research has shown ways in which social norms and moral dimensions are formulated and accounted for in the actual exchange of talk (e.g., Drew 1998; Maynard 1985; Pomerantz 1986; Mandelbaum 1993), and some have demonstrated ways in which social identities and relations are negotiated and achieved through interaction (e.g., Antaki and Widdicombe 2008; Hester and Eglin 1997a; Jefferson et al. 1987; Goodwin and Goodwin 1990; Mandelbaum 1987, 2003; Raymond and Heritage 2006). This line of research is inspired by Garfinkel's point of view that social life is a continuous display of members' local understandings of what is going on (Garfinkel 1967). It is also influenced by Sacks (1972), who suggested that people construe others and their activities by identifying sets of categories, which can be used in participants' explanation of themselves, or others, and their actions, and that certain activities can be treated as "bound" to certain categories and this boundedness provides a common-sense understanding of the world. It has been understood from these perspectives that linkages between the identities of actors and the nature of their actions in interaction are one of the central mechanisms by which social structure is produced, and that the ways in which identities are relevant for action-in-interaction constitute a basic link between individuals and social structure (Raymond and Heritage 2006). Social life is thus the business that people conduct with each other, displayed in their everyday practices, and social identities and relations are what participants create, define, negotiate, maintain, and therefore perform through interaction. Following this line of research, I also examine in this chapter how the participants relevantly embody particular social identities, relations, and memberships for the local contexts through the complaining activity.

5.1. SOCIAL IDENTITIES AND RELATIONS

5.1.1. Complaining as a Site of Constructing Social Identities and Relations

Schegloff (1991, 1992) has suggested that, in order to examine the connection between social characteristics such as gender, race, ethnicity, familial status, etc. and participants' conduct in interaction, it is necessary to identify and demonstrate the range of practices through which participants' particular features are made relevant and consequential in specific actions. According to him, characterizations of participants should be grounded in aspects of what is going on in interaction that are demonstrably relevant to the participants at the particular moment. This approach provides a way of explicating the specific mechanisms by which social identities are sustained and made consequential in particular episodes of interaction.

In my data corpus, I have found that various kinds of social identities and relationships arise and become relevant in and through the interaction. The numerous complaint utterances examined in the preceding chapters bear such instances. For example, Fragment (1) below, which is taken from a dinner conversation among five friends, shows how Young makes relevant particular social identities of her own to the local context. She is a social participant who has various identities such as Korean, female, graduate student, daughter, roommate, friend, etc., just to name a few. She chooses a particular one out of her numerous identities at the particular moment and selectively positions herself as a hostess of the dinner gathering in line 1, by issuing a ritualistic invitation for the meal beginning to Hoon.

(1) [Dinner Talk among Five Friends]

1   Young: 많:이 먹어:. hu

                ma:nhi mek-e:. hu

                "((to Hoon)) Eat a lo:t ((/Help yourself)) hu"

Social Organization in Complaining Activity 115

```
2      {(2.0)/ ((Young pours beverage into cup and Hoon opens beverage can))}
3   Hoon:     누나 많이 먹는데요,
              nwuna manhi mek-nuntey-yo,
              "Sister, ((I)) will eat a lot, but"
4      {(1.2)/ ((Hoon turns head toward kitchen))}
5   Hoon:     *°숟가락 좀 주(h)세(h)요(h).°*
              *°swutkalak com cwu(h)-sey(h)-yo(h).°*
              * *: ((stands up and goes to kitchen))
              "Please give me a spoon ((/silverware))."
6      (0.6)
7   Jeong:    °어:°
              °e:°
              "°O:h°"
8   Young:    ((laugh))=
9   Hoon:     =°으°=
              =°u°=
              "°uh°"
10→ Young:   =왜(h)    얜    젓갈    [ 안    줬어:]
              =way(h) yay-n ceskal an  [ cw-ess -e:]
              "((to Jeong)) Why didn't ((you)) give chopsticks ((/silver-
              ware)) to hi:m?"
11  Jeong:                            [>이상하다,<] 아까 *밥:
                                      [>isangha-ta,<] akka *pa:p
12            (놨)는데¿=                              *: ((standing up))
              (nwa-ss) -nuntey¿=
              ">((It)) is (strange),< ((I)) put ((it)) a little while ago ((beside))
              the rice, but ((then why))¿"
```

While Young's ritualistic invitation for the meal beginning in line 1 constructs her identity as a hostess of the gathering, it simultaneously positions Hoon as a guest. In turn, Hoon displays his orientation to the local identities that Young has just brought up, by requesting silverware in line 5. Then, Young's complaint toward Jeong in line 10 creates a new dimension within her already-established identity. Her complaint utterance directs the responsibility to her roommate Jeong, and thereby formulates Jeong as a co-hostess of the gathering who is particularly responsible for the complainable event. In other words, Young still maintains the identity of a hostess of the social gathering but specifies her identity as a hostess who does not have a duty of providing silverware to the guests. Jeong acknowledges her responsibility through her response saying that she thought she had placed silverware at Hoon's dinner setting, and through this acknowledging response, Jeong co-participates in establishing her and Young's identities as co-hosts with different duties.

Whereas Young and Jeong put themselves in the same position of co-hostesses of a social gathering in the fragment above, they create a hierarchy within that category and attain different hierarchical statuses from each other in the following fragment. They are in the process of cooking a stew for the dinner at the moment, and Young checks the condition of the stew in this fragment. After looking into the stew pot, she issues a complaint toward Jeong in line 1.

(2) [Dinner Talk among Five Friends]

((Young comes to the table and looks into the stew pot. Then she grabs a plate with a vegetable and puts some into the stew.))

1 → Young: *더 많이 늫지: 왜 요만큼 넜대:*

   te manhi nuh-ci: way yo-mankhum ne-ss-tay:

   * *: ((keep putting vegetable into the stew))

   "((You)) should've put mo:re. Why did ((you)) put this litt:le?"

2   {(0.5)/ ((Young keeps putting vegetable into the stew.))}

3   Young: 이쁨-- 의쁨[만] 강조했구나.

   ippum-- ippum[-ma]n kangcohay-ss-kwuna.

   * *: ((keep putting vegetable into the stew))

   "Pretti-- ((you)) were just emphasizing the prettiness ((of it)), right."

4   Jeong: [반--]

   [pan--]

   "Half--"

5   {(.)/ ((Young keeps putting vegetable into the stew.))}

6	Jeong:	*반씩 (.) 이따 (넣을)라구.*

pan-ssik (.) itta (neh-ul)lakwu.

* *: ((Young keeps putting vegetable into the stew.))

"Half (.) ((I)) was gonna put the other half later."

7	Young:	아: 그래?

a: kulay?

"O:h, really?"

8	(0.5)	
9	Jeong:	내가 언니 말을 충실하(게 받들어서)

nay-ka enni mal-ul chwungsilha(key pattul-ese)

"I loyally (obeyed) what you said and"

10	(.)	
11	Young:	어 그래:.

e kulay:.

"Oh, re:ally."

12	(0.5)	
13	Young:	어유: 정확하게 반이다:.

eywu: cenghwakhakey pan-i-ta:.

"*Eywu:* ((it)) is exactly ha:lf, ((you're right))!"

14	Jeong:	((chuckle))

The first sentence in line 1 ("((You)) should've put mo:re.") expresses Young's normative orientation of cooking the stew and characterizes Jeong's performance of putting a particular amount of vegetable into the stew as a failure to reach the norm. The following sentence ("Why did ((you)) put this litt:le?") thus implies that Jeong will not be able to provide a reasonable answer, and thereby does challenging and complaining about Jeong's performance. In these utterances, Young strongly displays her epistemic certainty with the use of the suffix -*ci*, which expresses the speaker's definite belief (H. S. Lee 1999), and the use of the question format, which conveys a strong reversed polarity assertion (Koshik 2003, 2005). Thereby, she claims to have sufficient competence and knowledge to cook the stew and to cast doubt on the addressee's cooking performance. Also, she does not wait for Jeong to remedy the problem but provides a remedy herself by putting more vegetable into the stew (lines 1 through 6). By amending the problem without giving a chance to the complainee, Young more clearly claims her authority to cook. Thus, she constructs an authoritative identity, namely, the main cook for the dinner gathering, through the particular action of complaining.

Young's authoritative identity, which has been locally constructed is oriented to and aligned with by Jeong, too. After presenting an account that she intended to put in the other half later (line 6), Jeong formulates her conduct as a result of obeying Young's direction (line 9). In this formulation, she uses words such as *chwungsilha* ("loyally") and *pattul* ("obey"), and thereby positions herself as a follower. Although it is her strategy to avoid the responsibility, she co-establishes a hierarchy within the category of hostesses. The complaining activity thus provides the participants with a sphere for not only negotiating accountability and responsibility of their conduct but also invoking their particular social identities.

In contrast to the complainee in Fragment (2) who aligns herself with the hierarchical identities evoked by the complainant, the complainee in the following fragment contests the complainant's proposal of particular identities. It is an excerpt from a pizza gathering hosted by a married couple Yun and Suh, and the wife complains to her husband regarding the amount of fruit that he has peeled for the guests.

(3) [Pizza Gathering]

1 {(1.5)/ ((Yun, the wife, sees Suh, her husband, put some peeled fruit onto a plate.))}

2 → Yun: 에게: 더 깎어:

eykey: te kkakk-e:

"Eykey: peel mo:re!"

3 → Suh: 더 깎을 거야:

te kkakk-ul ke-ya:

"((I)) WILL peel mo:re!"

Yun's complaint displays her orientation to Suh's local identity as a host of the social gathering who gets fruit ready for the guests to eat. Within this orientation, she points out his failure to prepare an appropriate amount, and thereby characterizes him as an incompetent host. At the same time, she represents herself as a co-host who is more competent. In other words, she embodies her identity as a co-host with better knowledge and hence the right to give him such a command and an order. However, such embodiment by

Yun is disputed by Suh's response. First, he refuses to be positioned as a complainee: He issues a counter-complaint, and thereby re-positions himself as a new complainant and Yun as a complainee. Also, by claiming that he was going to peel more fruit and hence she should not have criticized him, he rejects the framework of "more knowledgeable versus incompetent party host" suggested by Yun's preceding complaint.

Another kind of social identity is constructed through complaining in the following fragment. In this phone conversation between two high school girls, the caller Nami formulates herself as a close friend to Eun by complaining in lines 4 and 5.

(4) [Phone Conversation between Two High School Girls]

((Nami is calling her friend Eun.))

1 Eun: 여보세요:?

   yeposeyyo:?
   "Hello:?"

2 Nami: 나 나미다.

   na Nami-ta.
   "This is Nami."

3 Eun: 응:. 오랜만이네?

   u:ng. olayn-man-i-ney?
   "Yea:h. Long time no see!"

4→ Nami: **어찌 내가 전활 안 하면 전활**

   ecci nay-ka cenhwa-l an ha-myen CENHWA-L

5→   **한 통화도 안 하냐?**

   HAN THONGHWA-TO an ha-nya?
   "**How come ((you)) NEVER MAKE A <u>SINGLE PHONE CALL</u> ((to me)) if I don't call ((you))?**"

Nami's complaint presents a contrast between Eun's lack of communication and Nami's own efforts to maintain their relationship. It also evokes a social norm that a mutual effort to keep in touch regularly is necessary between friends. Nami's complaint, most importantly, is an embodiment of Nami's identity as a close friend who has the right to complain about Eun's lack of effort, and its sequential position contributes to the construction of this particular identity. It is produced immediately after Eun's recognition of and greeting to Nami ("Yea:h. Long time no see!"), that is, in the sequential position in which a responsive greeting is expected (cf., Schegloff 1986). By issuing the complaint even without returning a greeting to the call receiver, Nami suggests that the complained-of event is very urgent and important to bring up. Nami thus proposes that she is such an intimate friend that not having a phone conversation for a long time with Eun is a matter of great importance to urgently deal with.

As exemplified through Fragments (1) through (4), various kinds of social identities are procedurally embodied and made specifically relevant to the actions carried out at a particular moment in the course of interaction. The speakers' embodiment of their own identities also implies their social relations to others. The complainant Young invokes a social relation between herself and Jeong as co-members of the hosting party at the moment in Fragment (1) and as the main hosting party who is in charge of cooking and the assistant in Fragment (2), as discussed earlier. Yun in Fragment (3) proposes a social relation with her husband as the hosting party with better knowledge of how to serve guests, and the less competent hosting party, but the husband disputes it and evokes alternative identities as equally competent co-hosting parties. Nami in Fragment (4) also creates a social relation with Eun as close friends through her complaint. The complaints then point out that the complainees' target conduct has violated a certain norm shared within the particular social relations between the participants. Pointing out the violation of relational norms has social implications, which will be discussed in the next section.

5.1.2. Complaining for Social Solidarity

Given that complaining, specifically direct complaining, claims the addressee's conduct to have violated a shared norm, it operates as a "face-threatening act" (Brown and Levinson 1987). According to Brown and Levinson (1987), face-threatening acts, such as complaining, threaten the hearer's positive face in that they characterize the addressee's behavior as "wrong or misguided or unreasonable about some important issue, such wrongness being associated with disapproval" (67). In contrast, positive politeness strategies such as compliments, Brown and Levinson say, show the speaker's respect for the hearer's need and desire. Within this framework, positive politeness is regarded as solidarity-establishing behavior, whereas face-threatening acts are considered to distance social relationships.

However, it may be an oversimplification to say that positive politeness always contributes to social harmony and face-threatening acts are intrinsically associated with social distancing. Although it is true that complaining threatens the addressee's face by pointing out the offense of his or her target behavior, complaining can simultaneously provide a resource for creating social solidarity. The following fragment shows such an instance. It is taken from a phone conversation between high school girls who belong to a web community within their school. The members, except for Eun, are having a party at Jeon's place, and so Jeon is calling Eun and complains about her absence (lines 1 and 2), and Eun complains back toward Jeon about the failure to notify her of the party (lines 3 and 4).

(5) [Phone Conversation among High School Girls]

1 →Jeon: 야 오늘 우리 ㄷ-- 다 모여서 고기 구워먹기로

ya onul wuli t-- ta moy-ese koki kwuwe mek-ki-lo

2 → 했는데 너만 안 왔어:

hay-ss-nuntey ne-man an wa-ss-e:

"Hey we have decided to gather for a meat party a-- all together today, but you are the only one who hasn't co:me!"

((About 100 lines are deleted: see the subsequent fragments, (7), (8), and (9), for deleted lines))

3 →Eun: *이 자식들 나한테 그 연락 하나

*I CASIK-TUL. .h NA-HANTHEY KU YENLAK HANA

4 → 못 하냐?*

MOS HA-NYA?*   * *: ((pretending-anger voice))

"THESE JERKS. .h ((YOU)) COULDN'T EVEN CONTACT ME?"

In her complaint, Jeon contrasts Eun with "all" the other members who are present, with the use of the contrastive connective *-nuntey* (Choi 1991) and two linguistic elements *ta* ("all") and *-man* (a particle meaning "only"). Also, she brings up the issue of membership, by saying that it was the community's decision to have the gathering, and formulates Eun's absence as a failure to do being a member of the community. On the other hand, Eun explicitly points out that all the other members, instead of Jeon only, are to blame for not giving her notice, through the address term, *I CASIK-TUL* ("THESE JERKS"). Thus, Jeon and Eun establish the relevance of group membership through their complaints, and thereby construct their social relationship as co-members of the group.

The complaints by Jeon and Eun can be distancing to their social relationship in that they formulate each other's target behavior as an offense against harmoniously maintaining their membership. However, at the same time, the participants use the action of complaining in order to maintain their membership and friendship. First, through Jeon's complaint, Eun's presence at the party becomes a very important matter. That is, Jeon displays by complaining that she cares about Eun's presence and hence that Eun is a member of great importance. Jeon indeed expresses her feeling in the later talk through an utterance, "*ai:* I wish you were he:re!" (see line 59 in Fragment (9) in the following section, 5.2). On the other hand, Eun's complaint formulates the party as a significant matter to her. It is so significant that she minds not being informed of it in advance. If she had not complained, it would have meant that she did not have any interest in the gathering, which might have been an offense to their group solidarity. She expresses more explicitly her interest in the gathering through another complaint in the later talk, ">(What are you guys doing)< HEY: JUST AMONG YOURSELVES ((WITHOUT ME)) LIKE(h) THAT(h) (.) *a*(h)*i* darn(h).") (see lines 38 and 39 in Fragment (8) in 5.2). The complaints by Jeon and Eun are thus associated with high solidarity and exhibit the speakers' desire that the hearer should feel wanted, appreciated, and somehow part of the group, which is exactly what Brown and Levinson (1987) consider to be the feature of positive politeness strategies.

Complaining, then, cannot simply be explained as a face-threatening act which constantly causes harm to social harmony and bonds. Its social implications and consequences are so complex that simply associating it to be face-threatening and social distancing could not elucidate diverse cases of complaining. The social implications should thus be accounted for in actual episodes of interaction based on the specific aspects that the participants make relevant to their ongoing actions at particular moments.

5.2. MEMBERSHIP CATEGORIZATION AND ORIENTING TO NORMS FOR *GOOD* CATEGORY MEMBERS

By embodying identities through complaining, the participants not only create social relations among themselves but also invoke membership categorization. For example, the participants in Fragment (5) in the preceding section treat each other as co-members of a certain group and thereby construct a particular kind of membership that they share, which will be shown in the subsequent analysis. This particular membership does not exist as a decontextualized conception that provides a basis for explaining the participants' practices. On the contrary, the meaning or sense of the membership category is occasioned, negotiated, and accomplished through the participants' conversational practices in the ongoing interaction (Hester and Eglin 1997b). This section demonstrates, by analyzing an extended version of Fragment (5) and another conversation in detail, how social participants propose, negotiate, and achieve their membership categories through the interactional activity of complaining.

First, in the phone conversation among high school girls, membership categorization is raised as an important issue from the beginning by the participants. As mentioned earlier, Jeon is calling Eun in this fragment while having a gathering at her place with other members of a web community within their school. In the immediately preceding context, a family member of Eun's answered the phone and switched to her. The talk between Jeon and Eun starts in line 1 below.

(6) [Phone Call among High School Girls]

1 Jeon: (야)

 (ya).
 "(Hey you)."

2 Eun: *누구야.* * *: ((scared voice))

 nwukwu-ya.
 "Who is this?"

3 Jeon: 전이.

 Jeoni.
 "((This is)) Jeoni."

4 Eun: *어:* * *: ((scared voice))

 e:.
 "Yea:h."

5 Jeon: 야. 너:, 으-- 안 들어와?=마당?

 ya. ne:, u-- an tulewa?=matang?
 "Hey. You:, uh-- haven't you checked lately? ((Our website)) Matang?"
 ((Literally: "Don't you come in? ((Into our website)) *Matang?*"))

6   (0.6)
7   Eun: 왜:?

   way:?
   "Why:?"

8 →Jeon: 야 오늘 우리 ㄷ-- 다 모여서 고기 구워먹기로

   ya onul wuli t-- ta moy-ese koki kwuwe mek-ki-lo

9 →   했는데 너만 안 왔어:

   hay-ss-nuntey ne-man an wa-ss-e:
   "Hey we have decided to gather for a meat party a-- all together today, but you are the only one who hasn't co:me!"

10   (.)
11→Jeon: 너 야: 연락이 안 돼서:,=

   ne ya: yenlak-i an tway-se:,=
   "Hey, because you couldn't be reached,"

From the very beginning of the phone conversation, Jeon's unfavorable stance is conveyed to Eun even though the utterance in line 1, *(ya).* "(Hey you).," is very short and unclear. One of the functions of *ya* is a vocative token (like "hey" in English), and it often expresses the speaker's upset state of mind. The utterance with an unfavorable tone is a type of prospective indexical (Goodwin 1996).[1] It projects an unfriendly forthcoming action (the upcoming action of complaining in lines 8 and 9), and puts the recipient Eun in the position of having to monitor further talk in order to determine what exactly the hostile quality is indicating. Eun thereupon displays her orientation to the caller's unfavorable stance with the use of "scared voice" while requesting the caller to identify herself ("Who is this?" in line 2). Eun uses the same frightened voice in acknowledging the caller's identification in line 4. After the identification sequence, Jeon issues a question in line 5 regarding whether Eun has checked their website lately, and thereby indicates that the reason for the call is related to Eun's participation in their web community. In doing so, Jeon mentions the name of the web community (*Matang*) which she and Eun belong to and thereby brings up the relevance of this particular membership to what they are talking about. Also, she indicates with the use of the verb *tulewa* ("come in") that she is inside the boundary of the community but that the addressee Eun is outside the boundary, at the moment. Given that Eun is also a member, Jeon's utterance implies that something is going on in the community at that point in time and that she has detected that Eun does not seem to know about it because she has not checked the website lately. In this way, Jeon establishes the membership in that particular community as the important issue for the phone conversation.

In subsequent talk, Jeon explicates the unfavorable stance that she displayed at the beginning: She issues a complaint in lines 8 and 9 about Eun not attending the party ("Hey we have decided to gather for a meat party a-- all together today, but you are the only one who hasn't co:me!"). In this complaint, she emphasizes that the party was the community's decision, and highlights the contrast between "all" the other members (*ta*) who are present and "only Eun" (*ne-man*, "you only") who is absent from the party. She further formulates Eun as the attributable party of the failure in communication (line 11): She forms the utterance with the use of *ne* ("you," in this case Eun) as the subject in the passive sentence format ("you couldn't be reached"), instead of saying "we couldn't reach you" with the use of "we" as the subject. By utilizing the passive sentence, Jeon "foregrounds" *ne* ("you") as an important piece of information to be highlighted (cf. Chafe 1976). Foregrounding is a linguistic strategy which gives prominence to a linguistic element and makes it more meaningfully significant, and passivization of an active sentence is a means of foregrounding. Jeon utilizes the strategy of foregrounding *ne* in order to put emphasis on the responsibility of the addressee Eun. With the use of foregrounding and the other turn resources, Jeon formulates Eun's absence as a failure of "doing being a proper member of the community," a complainable act from the perspective of the other members.

The issue of being a proper member is treated as a matter of importance in the subsequent complaints and responses as well. In line 20, Eun makes an account of why she cannot come to the party, which is that she has a tutoring session. Jeon then produces another complaint that Eun studies too hard in line 21.

(7) [Phone Call among High School Girls]

12 Eun: 어딘데.

　　　　　　eti-ntey.
　　　　　　"Where ((are you having the party))?"

13 (.)

14 Jeon: 우리 집이지.

　　　　　　wuli cip-i-ci.
　　　　　　"My place, of course."

15 (.)

16 Eun: 아, 나 못 가↑

         a, na mos ka↑
         "Ah, I can't go↑"
17 (.)
18 Jeon: 왜.

         way.
         "Why."
19 (0.5)
20 Eun: 나?°으 ㅈ° 과외 있어:. 다섯 시에.=

         na? °u c° kwaoy iss-e:. tases si-ey.=
         "Me? °u c° ((I)) have a tutoring session. At five o'clock."=
21→Jeon: **=아 이 새끼 공부 열(h)라(h) 열(h)심(h)히(h) 해(h) .h**

         =*a i saykki kongpwu yel(h)la(h) yel(h)sim(h)hi(h) hay(h) .h*
         ="Ah this jerk, ((you)) study too(h) hard(h) .h"
22 (.)
23 Jeon: *↑아::↑ (0.5) 기달려봐?

         *↑*a::↑* (0.5) *kitally-epwa?*
         * *: ((It sounds like she just got hurt by stepping or bumping to
                 something.))
         "↑Ouch↑ (0.5) Wait a minute?"

((About ten lines deleted: Jeon switches the phone to Yeon, another participant at the gathering, and Yeon identifies herself to Eun))

24 Eun: 오랜만이네¿

         olaynman-i-ney¿
         "It's been a while, right¿"
25 Yeon: 어:.

         e:.
         "Ye:s."
26 (0.5)
27 Eun: 응:.

u:ng.
"Ye:s."

28 →Yeon: 공부 열심히 하는구나.

kongpwu yelsimhi ha-nun-kwuna.
"((You)) seem to be studying hard."

29 →Eun: 아니 그게 아니야.

ani ku-key ani-ya.
"No that's not it."

30 (0.5)

31 Yeon: 그러면은?

kulemyen-un?
"Then ((what is it))?"

32 →Eun: 까먹구 있었어.=야: °아° ↑한참 안 들어왔잖아

kkamek-kwu iss-ess-e.=ya: °a° ↑hancham an tulewa-ss-canh-a

33 → 학기 중에는:.↑

hakki-cwung-ey-nu:n.↑
"I <u>forgot</u>.=He:y °a° ↑((I)) haven't checked ((the website)) for a long time, you know. In the middle of semester ((we don't)).↑"

34 (0.5)

35 Yeon: °어::° (0.8) °그런 거구나.°=

°e::° (0.8) °kule-n ke-kwuna.°=
"°O::h° (0.8) °That was it.°"=

36 Eun: =음:.

=u:m.
="Yea:h."

In her complaint in line 21, Jeon first issues a response cry (*a*), which often projects a forthcoming complaint and addresses Eun as *i saykki* ("this jerk")[2], a form of insult. Then, she describes Eun's studying as an excessive act with the use of an adverb *yella*, which is an intensifying slang term meaning "very" often with a negative implication. Although the laugh tokens within this utterance lighten the tone, it clearly formulates Eun's target act as an improperly extreme one. Since this complaint is produced in response to Eun's account-giving, it operates as a resource for rejecting the account, and for further blaming Eun for not joining the group because of a study schedule.

Eun does not immediately react, but she displays her orientation to the complaint of turning down the group in order to study, in the later talk when another member makes a comment similar to Jeon's. After line 23, Jeon switches the phone to Yeon, another participant at the party, and when Eun and Yeon complete a greeting sequence (lines 24 through 27), Yeon mentions Eun's studying (line 28). Since Yeon's utterance is only a comment about Eun's studying, Eun's response in line 29 can be heard as merely a denial of studying hard. However, when she elaborates on her denial in the subsequent talk upon Yeon's request, she gives an account explaining why she has not checked their website lately (lines 32 and 33). This shows that she has heard Yeon's comment on studying in line 28 as an interpretation of the reason of her absence and a complaint about it. In this account, Eun first says that she was in a forgetful state and then adds with a rush that she has not checked the website because it is now the middle of the semester when they see and talk to one another at school. That is, this is an account of why she has not been aware of the gathering. Whereas Yeon has only made a comment that Eun must have been studying very hard, Eun responds to it with an account as if responding to an explicit complaint.

In fact, her account is more directly related to the preceding complaints issued by the original caller Jeon. In the earlier talk, Jeon asked Eun if she had not checked their website recently (line 5 in (6)) and then complained that she was missing from the group ("Hey we have decided to gather for a meat party a-- all together today, but you are the only one who hasn't co:me!" in lines 8 and 9) and that she is not coming to the party because of studying ("Ah this jerk, ((you)) study too(h) hard(h) .h" in line 21 in (7)). Eun's account of why she has not checked the website and not been aware of the party thus refers to Jeon's complaints more directly than Yeon's comment. What Eun does is then giving an account directed toward Jeon's earlier complaints at the sequential position in which she is supposed to respond to Yeon's comment. In this way, she displays her interpretation of Yeon's comment as a continuation of the complaining action initiated earlier by Jeon. In other words, she treats Jeon and Yeon as a collective party who are complaining together about her unavailability and absence.

In the following talk, Eun continues to treat the other members as a collective party by formulating their act as "excluding her," and counter-complains about it (lines 38 and 39):

Social Organization in Complaining Activity   129

(8) [Phone Call among High School Girls]

```
37    (0.8)
38→Eun:    >(뭐 하기야)< 야: 니네끼리 그(h)렇(h)게(h)

           >(mwe ha-ki-ya)< YA: NINEY-KKILI KU(h)LEH(h)KEY(h)
39→        ( . ) 아(h)이(h) 씨(h). .h

           ( . ) a(h)i(h) ssi(h). .h
           ">(What are ((you)) doing)< HEY: JUST AMONG YOUR-
           SELVES ((WITHOUT ME)) LIKE(h) THAT(h) ( . ) a(h)i(h)
           darn(h). .h"
40    Yeon:    아 전이가 너한테(두) 어제 전화했는데

           a Jeoni-ka ne-hanthey-(twu) ecey cenhwayhay-ss-nuntey
41         학원 갔다구 그러던데?

           hakwen ka-ss-takwu kule-te-ntey?
           "Oh Jeon said she called you yesterday, too, but you were not
           home because you were gone to study at the learning center, you
           know?"
42    Eun:    아::, 늦게 전화했구나 그 [녀석두.]

           a::, nuckey cenhwayhay-ss-kwuna ku [nyesek-twu.]
           "O::h, ((she)) must have called ((me)) late, that kid ((/Jeoni))."
43    Yeon:                                  [°어:   ]:.° 그래:. (0.5) 전일

                                             [°e :   ]:.° kulay:. (0.5) Jeoni-l
44         탓 을 해.=

           thas-ul hay.=
           "°Yea::h.° Ri:ght. (0.5) Blame Jeoni."
45    (Jeon):    ↑어:?↑

           ↑e:?↑
           "↑Hu:h?↑"
46    (    ):    ((lau [gh))
47    Eun:       [그래. 쟤 탓을 해. 그냥.

              [kulay. cyay thas-ul hay. kunyang.
              "Right. ((I)) just blame her."
```

48	Yeon:	응:. 잠깐만.
		u:ng. camkkan-man.
		"Yea:h. Just a moment."
49	Eun:	°으:.° 음:.
		°u:° u:m.
		"°U:h° Okay."

Eun's complaint in lines 38 and 39 formulates the event of having a community party without Eun's presence as the other members' act of leaving her out (">(What are ((you)) doing)< HEY: JUST AMONG YOURSELVES ((WITHOUT ME)) LIKE(h) THAT(h) (.) *a*(h)*i*(h) darn(h). .h") whereas Jeon's earlier complaint has characterized the same event as Eun's act of not participating ("Ah this jerk, ((you)) study too(h) hard(h) .h"). Through her complaint, Eun expresses her displeasure about the party going on without her, thereby claiming that she wishes she had been included. Upon Eun's complaint, Yeon provides an account, on behalf of Jeon, of why they could not reach Eun (lines 40 and 41): Jeon called Eun the preceding day, but she was not home, gone to study at a private learning center. In her response, Eun attributes the failure to get the phone call to the specific time that Jeon chose to call (line 42).

Then Jeon reclaims the phone and negotiates the accusation laid on herself, as seen in Fragment (9): Jeon mentions another group member as the person responsible for notifying Eun ("*Au* Shin Hyun said she didn't know your phone number. So, she was not able to contact you, she said." in lines 54 and 55). However, Eun does not acknowledge that Jeon is free from blame. Instead, she issues another complaint that all the participants at the gathering are blameworthy (".h pht:: h (0.8) So ridiculous. h All of you. h" in line 56). In this way, Eun displays that she is concerned about the members' having a party without her, rather than about which individual member is responsible for the failure to contact her. That is, she sticks to the position of complaining about being excluded by the other members and thereby expresses her strong wish to be included as an in-group member.

(9) [Phone Call among High School Girls]

50	(0.5)	
51	Jeon:	여부쇼.
		yeppwusyo.
		"Hello. ((/*Blunt ending*))"

52 (.)
53 Eun: 어. 어.

           e. e.
           "Yeah. Yeah."

54→Jeon: 아으 <u>신현</u>이 니네 집 전화 번호 모른대,

           au <u>Shin</u> Hyun-i ni-ney cip cenhwa penho molu-ntay,
55→   그래서 연락을 못 했대.

           penho molu -ntay. kulayse yenlak-ul mos hay-ss-tay.
           "*Au <u>Shin</u> Hyun said she didn't know your phone number. So she was not able to contact you, she said.*"

56→Eun: .h 체:: h (0.8) 웃기고 있어. h 다들. h

           .h chey:: h (0.8) wuski-ko iss-e. h ta-tul. h
           ".h pht:: h (0.8) So ridiculous. h All of you. h"

57 Jeon: hh 어?

           hh e?
           "hh Huh?"

58 Eun: 다들 웃기고 있다구.=그래서 누구 누구 모였냐?

           ta-tul wuski -ko iss-takwu.=kulayse nwukwu nwukwu moy-ess-nya?
           "I said all of you are ridiculous.=So who exactly are there?"

((About twenty lines deleted: talking about who are present at the gathering))
59 Jeon: .h 아이: 아쉽다:,

           .h ai: aswip-ta:,
           ".h *ai:* I wish you were here!" ((literally: "I feel lacking!"))

60 Eun: 뭐가::.

           mwe-ka::.
           "Of wha::t."

61 (0.5)
62 Jeon: °*오빠* 너무해.° [아이 (   )--]

           °*oppa nemwuhay.*° [*ai* (   )--]
           "°*Brother*, you are not fair.° *Ai* (   )--"

* *: The community members playfully use *oppa* ("brother") to address Eun although she is a girl.

63 Eun: [정희-- 정]희두 희한하네.

[*Junghee-- Jung*]*hee-twu hihanha-ney* .

"Junghee-- Junghee was also unexpected ((to be there))."

((7 turns are deleted: comments on Junghee))

64→Eun: 야 그래서 니네끼리 고길 구워 먹는단 말야?

ya kulayse. ni-ney-kkili koki-l kwuwe mek nun-ta-n mal-ya?

"Hey, so. You guys are having a meat party without me, right?"

65 Jeon: 응:.

u:ng.

"Ye:s."

66 (0.8)

67→Eun: 따른 반도 아닌(데. h)

ttalun pan-to ani-(ntey. h)

"Even though ((we)) are in the same class. h"

68 Jeon: 뭐:, 오빠;, >오빠가 연락이 안됐잖아.<

MWE:, OPPA:, >oppa-ka yenlak-i an tway-ss-canha.<

"WHA:T, BRO:THER, >it was you who couldn't be contacted.<"

69 (1.5)

70→Eun: *이 자식들. .h 나한테 그 연락 하나

**I CASIK-TUL. .h NA-HANTHEY KU YENLAK HANA*

71→   못 하냐?*

MOS HA-NYA?   * *: ((pretending-anger voice))

"THESE JERKS. .h ((YOU)) COULDN'T EVEN CONTACT ME?"

72 Jeon: .h 아니 나는, 쟤:가 니네 집 전화 번호 아는데 니가

.h ani na-nu:n, cyay:-ka niney cip cenhwa penho a-nuntey ni-ka

73 연락이 안 되는줄 알았어.=근데 어제 전화해서: .h

yenlak-i an toy-nun cwul al-ass-e.=kuntey ecey cenhwahay-se: .h

74 은이 전화 번호 몰라?=그러니까:, ((continuing her account))

Euni cenhwa penho molla?=kule-nikka:,

".h No, I thought she ((/Shin Hyun)) knew your phone number ((and called you)) but it was you who were not available.=But when I called her yesterday .h and asked, 'don't you know Eun's phone number?' and she said . . ." ((continuing her account))

Eun's utterance in line 64 ("Hey, so. You guys are having a meat party without me, right?") is a more explicit complaint about the party going on without her. She even intensifies the complainability by pointing out that they could easily have informed her at school because they are in the same class ("Even though ((we)) are in the same class. h" in line 67). Jeon attempts to put the responsibility back on Eun again ("WHA:T, BRO:THER, >it was you who couldn't be contacted.<" in line 68), but Eun responds with another stronger complaint in lines 70 and 71 ("THESE JERKS. .h ((YOU)) COULDN'T EVEN CONTACT ME?"). She fortifies the other members' reprehensibility through the loud voice quality and the lexical choices of *CASIK-TUL* ("JERKS") and *HANA* ("NOT EVEN THE EASY THING TO DO").[3] Thereupon, Jeon changes her stance and starts to elaborate in line 72 how Shin Hyun held the main responsibility to notify Eun. In the later talk, which is not completely shown here due to the great lengthiness, Jeon reports to Eun that she came to know about Shin Hyun's failure to contact Eun only at the last minute and that is why she was not able to call her earlier. She displays, by giving this account, an agreement that Eun is not to blame for missing the gathering, and therefore Eun's effort to avoid the charge of neglecting the group ends up succeeding.

The participants in this talk-in-interaction occasion the group membership through the complaining activity. In the course of complaining, they characterize one another as the kind of girl who would rather study than have a party with friends, the incompetent messenger of the community gathering, the careless organizer of the gathering who has not checked on all the members' availability in advance, and the uncaring community members who are having a party with a member left out. In this way, they display their orientations to norms about what it means to be a responsible, caring member of the group, and also negotiate whether or not they conform to the norms. Thus, how they are characterized as proper or improper members is an achievement among the particular participants through their practical actions and reasoning in the local circumstances.

The following conversation also shows that membership categorization is an activity carried out in particular local circumstances. It is a conversation in which a three-year-old girl's mother complains toward the grandmother regarding her over-care for the child, as seen in (25) in 2.2.3. In Fragment (10) below, we have the preceding context to the mother's complaint. As background, Yun, a two-year-old boy's mother, is visiting Mijin's mother (Mom) and grandmother (Gran). They are neighbors in an apartment complex and have been friends through play-dates for the two children. Grandma has lived at Mijin's place since Mijin was born, and has helped Mom raise the child. In the following fragment, Yun brings up Mijin's baby sister Miun as a topic (line 1) and Mom and Grandma thereupon make comments about Miun that she is a more easygoing child than Mijin. Related to the comparison between Miun and Mijin, Yun directs the focus of the talk to Mijin and makes mention of some difficulties which she heard regarding Mijin ("You said Miji:n wildly .h started to (0.5) play wildly when she turned 100 days o:ld, right?" and "((She)) thrashed about. °u° Does ((she)) °no° longer" in lines 8 through 10). Through this confirmation-seeking remarks, Yun calls for the addressees' own views about the target event, and identifies both of them as Mijin's caregivers who have direct access to information about her.

(10) [Caregiver Talk]

1   Yun: 미은이가 미진이보다 더 순하다면[서요?]

        Miuni-ka Mijini-pota te swunha-ta-myens[e-yo?]
        "You said Miun is more easygoing than Mijin, right?"

2   Mom: [미]진이에

                                   [*Mi*]*jini-ey*

3   비하면:,=

        piha-mye:n,=
        "Compared to Miji:n,"=

4   Gran: =참 순해.

        =*cham swunhay.*
        ="((She)) is very easygoing."

((About 20 lines deleted: Gran elaborates how Miun is an easygoing baby.))

5	Mom:	언니한테 한 번 씩 맞으(h)믄(h) 울지 h [hu
		enni-hanthey han-pen-ssik mac-u(h)mun(h) wul-ci h [hu
		"If ((she)) gets hit by Mijin, then ((she))(h) cries(h), you know h hu"
6	Yun:	[((laugh))
7	(1.0)	
8	Yun:	미진이 백일 때:, 막 .h 그 때부터 막 (0.5) 장난
		Mijini payk -il ttay:, mak .h ku ttay pwuthe mak (0.5) cangnan
9		치기 시작했다 그러셨잖아요
		chiki sicakhay-ss-ta kule-sy-ess-canh-ayo
		"You said Miji:n wildly .h started to (0.5) play wildly when she turned 100 days o:ld, right?"
10		발버[둥치]구:, °으° [이젠 °안°]
		palpe[twungch]i-kwu:, °u° [icey-n °an°]
		"((She)) thrashed about. °u° Does ((she)) °no° longer"
11→	Gran:	[tch] [미진이]는: (0.8) 뭐 에려서
12→		[tch] [*Mijini*]-*nu:n (0.8) mwe eyly-ese* 부터 우는: 그 부터서 시작해가지구,=
		-pwuthe wu-nu:n ku pwuthese sicakhay-kacikwu,=
		"tch Miji:n (0.8) uh from the time ((she)) was a baby, ((she)) cried a lot and"
13→	Mom:	= °음° 개 콜릭 끼가 있어서:,
		=°*um° kyay colic-kki-ka iss-ese:,*
		= "°Yeah° because she had colic a li:ttle,"
14→	Gran:	마:: 이 또 [(설치기)를 시작]한께네:
		ma:: i tto [(selchi-ki) -lul sicak]ha-nkkeyney:
		"We::ll uhm ((she)) sta:rted (to behave uncontrollably)"
15→	Mom:	[너:무 많이 울°었어.°]
		[*ne:mwu manhi wul-°ess-e.°*]
		"She cried too: much."

Grandma confirms Yun's comments by beginning to give details of Mijin's problematical behavior (lines 11, 12, and 14), and Mom also shows her orientation to the child's difficulties by mentioning that she cried too much because of colic (line 13). Grandma identifies herself as Mijin's caregiver by giving details of Mijin's behavior that was hard to handle, and Mom embodies the same identity by adding another detail. Therefore, the participants' talk about Mijin's behavior generates a membership category of caregivers, and since Yun is also a mother of a two-year-old boy herself, the complaint about Mijin's difficulties is an invitation for her to join the group.

The membership of caregivers is maintained as a categorical framework in the subsequent talk as well. Grandma keeps talking about the unruly behavior which Mijin showed when she was younger, relates it to her current behavior (in line 16), and then gives more specific examples beginning with her undisciplined eating behavior (line 20). Mom makes a comment that Mijin's improper eating habit is caused by the grown-ups who spoil the child by going after and spoonfeeding her (lines 27 through 29), and then Yun also displays her orientation to the membership to the caregiver category by sharing her own difficulty with her child (lines 30, 32, 33, 35, and 36)[4]. In line 31, however, Mom specifies "the grown-ups," who spoil the child as "Grandma" and thereby directs the responsibility to her. Through Mom's specification of grown-ups as Grandma, Mom's earlier comment in lines 27 through 29 turns out to be a direct complaint toward Grandma.

(11) [Caregiver Talk]

((20 lines deleted after Fragment (10): Gran's telling sequence that describes Mijin's unruly behavior of raging around))

16 Gran: 많이 설치˚구˚ 그러께 지금도 설치지.

            manhi selchi-˚kwu˚ kule-kkey cikum-to selchi-ci.

            "Because ((Mijin)) behaved uncontrollably so much ((at that time)), ((she)) still does that, you know."

17 (0.5)

18 Yun: 네˚에.˚

            ney˚ey.˚

            "Yeah."

19 (1.0)

20 Gran: ↑밥을 앉아서 안 먹어요↑ 지금도:,

Social Organization in Complaining Activity 137

		↑*pap-ul <u>anc</u>-ase an mek-eyo*↑ *cikum-to:,*
		"↑((She)) doesn't <u>sit</u> still while <u>eating</u>↑ even no:w,"
21	(1.0)	
22	Gran:	°꼭:° 떠멕여가지고: °(그렁께)°

°kko:k° ttey-meyky-ekaciko: °(kulengkkey)°

"°every ti:me° ((we)) have to spoon up food and fee:d ((her)) °and so°"

| 23 | <밥 먹는 시간:> 뭐, .h <머리 빗는 시간:> |

<pap mek-nun sika:n> mwe, .h <meli pis-nun sika:n>

"<the time for ea:ting> and like, .h <the time for doing ((her)) hai:r>"

| 24 | 머리도 가마이 안 앉았응께 따라(댕기)면서 |

meli-to kamai an anc-ass-ungkkey ttala(tayngki)-myense

| 25 | 빗:긴다구 °저 에미(는)° .h 옷도 그러제: (1.5) |

pi:ski-nta-kwu °ce eymi-(nun)° .h os-to kule-cey: (1.5)

"((her)) hair, too, because ((she)) would not sit still, °her mom° has to follow ((her)) around, you know .h the same with ((her)) clo:thes (1.5)"

| 26 | >아들이 어디 [가(자구)하면<] |

>a-tul-i eti [ka-(cakwu)-ha-myen<]

">so if they say ((they)) (should) go somewhere then<"

| 27 | Mom: | [걔는 밥을] (0.3) °u° 당연히 안 앉아 먹게 |

          [kyay-nun pap-ul] (0.3) °u° tangyenhi an anc-a mek-key

| 28 | 돼 있어: 어른들이 *쫓아다니면서 먹이 |

tway-iss-e: elun-tul-i ccochatani-myense .h meki

| 29 | [니까*] |

[-nikka]   * *: ((laugh voice))*

"She has her meal (0.3) °u° it's no wonder she turns out not to sit still for ea:ting because grown-ups follow her around and spoonfeed her"

138   *Chapter 5*

30   Yun: [그러니깐:,] 집에 와서=

              [kule-nikka:n,] CIP-EY wa-se=
              "Because of tha:t, when ((my son)) gets HOME"

31→ Mom: =.h 할머니가 계::속   [쫓아다니면서 먹이는데:,]

              =.h halmeni-ka kyey::sok [ccochatani-myense (mek)i-nuntey:,]
              ".h Grandma follows her around and spoonfeeds ((her)) a::ll the time, and so"

32   Yun: [그러니까 °그게° 버릇이 °(그:)°] 돼

                                        [kule-nikka °ku-key° pelus-i °(ku:)°] tway

33   가지구:,=

              -kacikwu:,=
              "Because of that, °that° becomes °(u:h)° ((his)) habit, a:nd"

34→ Mom: =.h 걔가 왜 *와서 거기* 앉[아 있겠어:]

              =.h kyay-ka way *wa-se keki* anc[a iss-keyss-e:]
                              *   *: ((smile voice))
              ".h why would she come(h) and sit(h) still there, you kno:w"

35   Yun: [애가 누워가]지고는

                                              [ay-ka nwuwe-ka]ciko-nun

36   (자[기](h))

              (ca[ki(h)])
              "He lies down and(h)"

37   Mom: [아쉬운게 없는데[:,

              [aswiwun-key eps-nuntey[:,
              "Because there is nothing else ((she)) wants, you know"

38   Yun: [맞어:.

                                   [mac-e:.
              "Right."

In her complaint (".h Grandma follows her around and spoonfeeds ((her)) a::ll the time, and so .h why would she come(h) and sit(h) still there, you kno:w"), Mom describes Grandma's act of following Mijin around to spoonfeed her as an excessive one which occurs in a constant and regularized manner, and thereby she characterizes the complainee as "a grandmother who over-cares for and hence spoils the child." This complaint thus shows that Mom has different normative orientations about what a "good" caregiver is.

In response, Grandma gives an account as presented in the following fragment, and negotiates the meaning of the given membership category. In her account, Grandma tries to claim that there is no other way because the child does not eat otherwise, but Mom furthers her original complaint with an interruption by elaborating the way in which the child is spoonfed by Grandma (lines 40 and 41). Then, Grandma interrupts her in turn and clearly articulates, as an account, the reason that she uses the particular way of feeding the child (lines 45 and 46).

(12) [Caregiver Talk]

39→Gran: .h <안 먹어서 °(그래도)° 할[-- >

.h <*an mek-ese °(kulayto)° ha[-- >*

".h <Because she doesn't eat ((otherwise)). °(But)° there is no choice-->"

40 Mom: [>테레비 앞에 <u>가</u>만

[>*theyleypi aph-ey <u>ka</u>man*

41 앉아있어도 밥 숟가락이 샥: [들어오거덩¿<]

anc-aiss-eto pap swutkalak-i sya:k [tuleo-keteng¿<]

">Even when ((she)) is <u>ju</u>st sitting in front of TV, the food is automatically carried ((into her mouth)), you know¿<"

42 Yun: [((c h u c k] l e))
43 [((c h] u [c k l e))]
44 Mom: [hu 그(h)러(h)니까:,]

[*hu ku(h)le(h)nikka:,*]

"hu Because of tha:t,"

45→Gran: [그런데 밥 먹으러 <u>안</u> 오니까]

[*kulentey <u>pap</u> mek-ule <u>an</u> o-nikka*]

46→ °인제° 내가 가서 <u>먹</u>이니까.=

°*incey° nay-ka ka-se <u>meki</u>-nikka.=*

"But because she does <u>not come</u> to eat, that's why I go and <u>spoon</u>feed her."

| 47 | Yun: | =*그러니까 계:속 그게 악순환이지 뭐.*.h |

        =*<u>ku</u>lenikka kyey:sok ku-key akswunhwan-i-ci mwe.*.h
        *   *: ((smile voice))
        "Because of that, that becomes a vicious circle, you know. .h"

| 48 | Mom: | °그러니까:° |

        °*kulenikka:*°
        "°That's what ((I)) mea:n.°"

As for Yun, she displays different stances in the course of the complaining activity by affiliating with Mom at one point and with Grandma at another. For example, her comment about a vicious circle in line 47 displays her disapproval of Grandma's account and therefore affiliation with Mom. Yun talked about her son's undisciplined eating behavior before the participants started to talk about Mijin, and thus Yun's comment about a vicious circle in line 47 may have been about her own problem as a continuation of her preceding talk about her son. Whether or not it is the case, Mom's absolute agreement at the very moment (line 48, °*kule-nikka:*° "°That's what I mea:n.°") formulates it as a characterization of Grandma's act, and Yun and Mom thereupon become categorized as "good" caregivers while Grandma becomes a spoiling one. On the other hand, Yun affiliates with Grandma in the later talk by expressing her understanding of Grandma's conduct, which is presented in Fragment (13):

(13) [Caregiver Talk]

((7 lines deleted: immediately after (12), Yun makes a suggestion that they not give an afternoon-snack to Mijin until dinner time so that she would eagerly eat by herself at dinner.))

| 49 | Mom: | 어떤 때는:, 정:말 먹어요 막 지가:, |

        ETTUN TTAY-NU:N, <u>ce:ng</u>mal mek-eyo mak ci-ka:,
        "AT CERTAIN TI:MES, ((she)) eagerly eats. Really by herse:lf,"

| 50 | Yun: | °아:° |

        °*a:*°
        "°O:h°"

| 51 | (0.5) |

52	Mom:	.h 너무 배고플 때는:,
		.h nemwu paykophu-l ttay-nu:n,
		".h when ((she)) is really hu:ngry,"
53		(0.5)
54	Mom:	근데 (.) <u>그 순간</u>까지 엄마(h)는(h)
		kuntey (.) <u>ku swun</u>kan-kkaci emma(h)-nun(h)
55		못 기다리시(h)는(h)거(h)야(h) .h=
		mos kitali-si(h)-nun(h) ke(h)-ya(h) .h=
		"But (.) the thing is that my mom(h) is(h) not(h) able(h) to wait until that moment .h"=
56→	Yun:	=°으° 애 배고플텐[데]:,=
		=°u° ay paykophu-lthey-n[tey]:,=
		"°Yeah° Because ((she thinks)) the kid must be hungry,"
57	Mom:	[°어으°]
		[°*eu*°]
58→	Yun:	=[할머니 마음이]
		=[halmeni maum-i]
		"**Grandma's caring heart is**"
59	Mom:	[얼른 먹여야 된다]고 막 [이러면]은
		[ellun meky-eya toy-nta]ko mak [ile-myen]-un
		"If my mom eagerly says like we have to feed her q<u>u</u>ick"
60	Yun:	[.hh] 그렇구나:.
		[.hh] *kuleh-kwuna:.*
		".hh I see:."

After Yun makes a suggestion for disciplining the child, Mom utilizes it to advance her original complaint toward Grandma even further (lines 54 and 55). In response, Yun shows her understanding of why Grandma does the complained-about act (line 56), and then characterizes the reason as "grandma's caring heart" (line 58). However, it does not mean that she is agreeing with the ways in which Grandma takes care of the child. Nor does she sympathize with and join Mom in complaining against Grandma, but puts herself into a neutral position.

In sum, Grandma invokes a membership category of caregivers by complaining about her granddaughter and the other participants join in and share their difficulties of raising children. Then, Mom complains against Grandma regarding a specific discipline problem, and she and Grandma begin to negotiate the meanings of the good caregiver category. Yun first agrees with Mom that Grandma's way of spoonfeeding the child can spoil her, but later expresses her understanding of why Grandma does so. The participants in this conversation thus establish the membership among themselves by treating one another as co-members. All through the course of complaining activity, they display their orientations to norms for proper caregivers, and negotiate whether or not they are appropriate caregivers, by issuing complaints, providing accounts, or affiliating with other participants' opinions.

5.3. SUMMARY

This chapter has shown, through the analysis of complaining activities, how particular social identities and memberships are occasioned and moral norms are accounted for in the local contexts at the particular moments. The complainants embody various kinds of social identities and make them specifically relevant to the actions that they are carrying out in the course of interaction. The complainants' embodiment of their own identities also implies their social relations to others and the memberships which they share. By carrying out the complaining action, they point out that the target conduct has violated a certain norm shared among the group members. The complainants and the other participants, in order to achieve the status of proper member, then negotiate throughout the interaction whether or not they are operating according to the norms. My analysis of complaining therefore suggests that language use in the specific action operates as a resource for joining the participants together or keeping them apart in particular social ways, and that social organization is what the participants negotiate and collaboratively accomplish through their practical actions and reasoning in the local circumstances.

NOTES

1. According to Goodwin, in conversation speakers sometimes utilize a linguistic expression whose specification is not yet available at the moment, but instead must be discovered in the subsequent talk. As a representative example of such an expression, he mentions "story prefaces." For instance, when a speaker says, "The most terrible thing happened to me today!," this utterance determines the

recipient's task of paying attention to the following utterance in order to find what specific event is indexed by the expression, "the most terrible thing." Thus, a prospective indexical encourages recipients to attend to the following talk, engages them in an active process of discovering the specification of the indexical and accordingly reacting to it.

2. *Saykki* usually refers to a male. The particular participants in this conversation are often found to use terms designating males for one another playfully.

3. See Fragment (19) in 2.2.1 for an explanation on how *hana* is used for the meaning of "not even the easy thing to do."

4. It is not clear whether Yun is talking about her son in her utterances in this fragment since her son is not overtly mentioned as the principal character of the story. However, in the preceding talk, she talked about her son's spoiled eating habit caused by her constant feeding, as presented below. Her story in Fragment (11) is thus its repetition, done this time for sharing similar experiences with the other caregivers.

```
1    Gran:   지:가 인제 혼자서 밥 떠먹어예:
```
ci:-ka incey honcase pap tte mek-eyey:
'Does he eat well by himse:lf?"

```
2    (0.5)
3    Yun:    [ 에:. ]
```
[ey:.]
"Ye:s."

```
4    Gran:   [지윤이]는.
```
[Jiyuni]-nun.
"I mean Jiyun."

```
5    Yun:    학교에서는: (0.3) 잘 먹는데 집에 와서는 제가 자꾸 버릇이 .h
```
hakkyo-eyse-nu:n (0.3) cal mek-nuntey cip-ey wa-se-nun cey-ka cakkwu pelus-i .h=
"((He)) is good at schoo:l, (.3) but at home, I constantly, the habit is .h"=

```
6    Gran:   =응:=
```
=u:ng=
"Yea:h"

```
7    Yun:    =>제가 자꾸<   주는게    [버릇이어서]
```
=>cey-ka cakkwu< cwu-nun-key [pelus-i-ese]
"it becomes the habit >that I feed ((him))<"

8   Gran: [얼렁 먹]일라구 그냥=

                                       [*elleng meyk*]*i-llakwu kunyang*=
   "Because ((we)) just want to feed ((them)) fast"

9   Yun: =에:

           =*ey:*
           "Ye:s"

Chapter 6

Concluding Remarks

This book has examined the ways in which Korean speakers manage a complaining activity to negotiate complainability in a variety of interactional contexts, with the aim of providing insight into the intertwined relationship between coordinated social interaction and sociocultural order. It has examined describing and reasoning practices employed for formulating complainability out of the target behavior or event (chapter 2), and linguistic resources recurrently used to initiate and construct complaints (chapter 3). It has also explicated organizational features of the whole complaining activity from the initial stage of complaints to the next responses and the closing of the entire activity (chapter 4). Another important goal of this study has been to analyze how the participants relevantly embody particular social identities and memberships through the complaining activity and thereby suggest that social organization is interactively negotiated and constituted through specific actions in the ongoing interaction (chapter 5).

The analysis of complaints in this book suggests pedagogical implications for teaching language and culture. Many researchers and practitioners agree that the goal of language teaching is to equip learners with communicative competence (Hymes 1967) and interactional competence (Young 2008) so that they can comprehend various types of linguistic, pragmatic, cultural, and interactional resources and communicate effectively in the target language. To successfully accomplish communicative and interactional goals, learners should be guided to understand what is meant by the words and expressions they hear and see and what kinds of social actions are carried out through them, and to be able to respond to them appropriately so that miscommunication can be avoided. Therefore, valid descriptions of practices through which native speakers accomplish social actions with language should be available to teachers and materials writers for effective teaching. Native speakers, although perfectly competent in the usage and interpretation of the patterns of speech behavior, are not aware of the patterned nature of their own speech behavior, and therefore native speaker intuitions are not necessarily adequate tools of description (Wolfson 1983). Some researchers consider natural data to have much greater potential to adequately describe the native language usage than self-report or intuition (e.g., McCarthy 1991; Wolfson 1983). Wolfson (1983, 4) states that "speech is best studied within the framework of the context in which it occurs" and therefore "nothing can replace the investigation of speech as it actually takes place." Due to the great demand for investigation using natural data, the analysis in this book can be of great benefit to Korean language teaching and material development, since it provides the educators with valid descriptions of how and why the complaining activity is done in natural settings.

Complaining has been treated as a unidirectional action done by the speaker in much of the research conducted within the framework of speech act theory (e.g., Olshtain and Weinbach 1987; Moon 1996; Murphy and Neu 1996), and a common presupposition of such research has been that complaining, especially direct complaining, is a face-threatening act (Brown and Levinson 1987) whose social function is to threaten the atmosphere of social harmony. However, as demonstrated and discussed in this book, complaining is an activity which the complainant and other participants conjointly accomplish through the interaction and by which the participants can locally construct various social identities and relationships, including positive ones. Therefore, whereas previous research presents simplified characteristics of complaining, this volume offers broader knowledge of the action in terms of its complex aspects so that its intricate characteristics can be properly understood by language educators and learners.

Complaining is a delicate action which speakers do not engage in lightly (Heinemann and Traverso 2009), and explicit complaint-devices such as "extreme case formulations" are only employed when a potential complaint has failed to receive appropriate uptake (Pomerantz 1986). Since complaints require delicacy and careful negotiation about the complainability, it benefits learners to consider the extent of complaints they would want to conduct depending on particular situations. Learners will also benefit by learning the variety of resources they can utilize in complaints in those particular situations. In addition, they can learn how to respond to complaints when they are positioned as direct complainees or recipients of indirect complaints. While complaining is not typically a focus for language learners as more "fundamental" actions such as greetings, seeking information, requests, invitations, and so on, my data show that complaining is frequently done in everyday life, and can contribute to building harmonious social relationships among participants. Therefore, information on patterns of complaining in native language use and its social implications could help learners appropriately interpret complaint utterances and respond exactly the way they choose to.

The analysis of complaining in this book also reveals some information concerning underlying sociocultural assumptions and values among Korean native speakers, since the complaining activity involves the participants' judgments of particular events. As many scholars have emphasized, language is a social practice that expresses cultural reality (Kramsch 1998), and language teaching is, by its very nature, concerned with understanding and interpreting cultural meaning (Wolfson 1983). Given the interwoven relationship between language and culture, information on sociocultural norms and values provided in this book through the Korean participants' complaining activities can contribute to learners' understanding of the community, and to the development of their communicative, interactional, and intercultural competence.

This book offers some possible directions for future research. First, cross-linguistic or cross-cultural research on complaining in terms of the various aspects investigated in this book would enhance our understanding of its patterns and social functions in different language communities. Second, whereas the present volume has examined how the complained-of event is described so that its complainability becomes outstanding and highlighted, it would be worthwhile to investigate mitigating practices employed in complaining to prevent its development into an acrimonious argument. Also, it would be of great interest to expand the contexts to interactions between professionals and clients in a variety of institutional settings, such as the interaction between service-providers and customers, teachers and students, and doctors and patients. The findings noted in this book provide a resource for future research on the variety of dynamic aspects of a complaining activity in numerous contexts.

Bibliography

Antaki, Charles, and Sue Widdicombe. 2008. *Identities in Talk*. London: SAGE Publications.
Balaji, M. S., Subhash Jha, and Marla B. Royne. 2015. "Customer E-Complaining Behaviours Using Social Media." *Service Industries Journal* 35 (11–12): 633–654. DOI: 10.1080/02642069.2015.1062883.
Boxer, Diana. 1993a. *Complaining and Commiserating: A Speech Act View of Solidarity in Spoken American English*. New York, NY: Peter Lang.
———. 1993b. "Complaints as Positive Strategies: What the Learner Needs to Know." *TESOL Quarterly* 27 (2): 277–299.
Brown, Penelope, and Stephen C. Levinson. 1987. *Politeness: Some Universals in Language Usage*. Cambridge: Cambridge University Press.
Chafe, Wallace L. 1976. "Givenness, Contrastiveness, Definiteness, Subjects, Topics, and Point of View." In *Subject and Topic*, edited by Charles N. Li, 245–269. New York: Academic Press.
Choi, Jaehee. 1991. *Kwukeui Cepsokmwun Kwuseng Yenkwu [Studies on the Structure of Korean Connectives]*. Seoul: Thapchwulphansa.
Clift, Rebecca. 2012. "Identifying Action: Laughter in Non-Humorous Reported Speech." *Journal of Pragmatics* 44 (10): 1303–1312.
———. 2016. "Don't Make Me Laugh: Responsive Laughter in (Dis)Affiliation." *Journal of Pragmatics* 100: 73–88.
Coulter, Jeff. 1990. "Elementary Properties of Argument Sequences." In *Interaction Competence*, edited by George Psathas, 181–203. Lanham, MD: University Press of America.
Dersley, Ian, and Anthony Wootton. 2000. "Complaint Sequences Within Antagonistic Argument." *Research on Language & Social Interaction* 33 (4): 375–406.
Drew, Paul. 1998. "Complaints About Transgressions and Misconduct." *Research on Language & Social Interaction* 31 (3 & 4): 295–325.
Ford, Cecilia E., Barbara A. Fox, and Sandra A. Thompson. 2002. *The Language of Turn and Sequence*. New York, NY: Oxford University Press.

Gardner, Rod. 2001. *When Listeners Talk: Response Tokens and Listener Stance*. Amsterdam: John Benjamins.

Garfinkel, Harold. 1967. *Studies in Ethnomethodology*. Englewood Cliffs, NJ: Prentice-Hall.

Goffman, Erving. 1981. *Forms of Talk*. Philadelphia, PA: University of Pennsylvania Press.

Goodwin, Charles. 1994. "Professional Vision." *American Anthropologist* 96: 606–633.

———. 1996. "Transparent Vision." In *Interaction and Grammar*, edited by Elinor Ochs, Emanuel A. Schegloff, and Sandra A. Thompson, 370–404. Cambridge; New York: Cambridge University Press.

Goodwin, Charles, and Marjorie H. Goodwin. 1990. "Interstitial Argument." In *Conflict Talk: Sociolinquistic Investigations of Arguments in Conversations*, edited by Allen Grimshaw, 85–117. Cambridge: Cambridge University Press.

Heinemann, Trine, and Véronique Traverso. 2009. "Complaining in Interaction." *Journal of Pragmatics* 41 (12): 2381–2384.

Heritage, John. 1984a. "A Change-of-State Token and Aspects of Its Sequential Placement." In *Structures of Social Action: Studies in Conversation Analysis*, edited by John M. Atkinson and John Heritage, 299–345. Cambridge: Cambridge University Press.

———. 1984b. *Garfinkel and Ethnomethodology*. Cambridge: Polity Press.

———. 2002. "The Limits of Questioning: Negative Interrogatives and Hostile Question Content." *Journal of Pragmatics* 34 (10–11): 1427–1446.

Heritage, John, and John M. Atkinson. 1984. "Introduction." In *Structures of Social Action: Studies in Conversation Analysis*, edited by George Psathas, 1–15. Cambridge: Cambridge University Press.

Heritage, John, and Rod Watson. 1979. "Formulations as Conversational Objects." In *Everyday Language: Studies in Ethnomethodology*, edited by George Psathas, 123–162. New York: Irvington Press.

Hester, Stephen, and Peter Eglin. 1997a. *Culture in Action: Studies in Membership Categorization Analysis*. Washington, DC: International Institute for Ethnomethodology and Conversation Analysis & University Press of America.

———. 1997b. "The Reflexive Constitution of Category, Predicate and Context in Two Settings." In *Culture in Action: Studies in Membership Categorization Analysis*, edited by Stephen Hester and Peter Eglin, 25–48. Washington, DC: International Institute for Ethnomethodology and Conversation Analysis & University Press of America.

Holt, Liz. 2012. "Using Laugh Responses to Defuse Complaints." *Research on Language & Social Interaction* 45 (4): 430–448.

Hymes, Dell. 1967. "Models of the Interaction of Language and Social Setting." *Journal of Social Issues* 23 (2): 8–28.

Jefferson, Gail. 1981. *The Abominable "Ne?": A Working Paper Exploring the Phenomenon of Post-Response Pursuit of Response*. Occasional Paper 6. Manchester: Department of Sociology, University of Manchester.

———. 1984. "On the Organization of Laughter in Talk About Troubles." In *Structures of Social Action: Studies in Conversation Analysis*, edited by John M. Atkinson and John Heritage, 346–369. Cambridge: Cambridge University Press.

———. 1988. "On the Sequential Organization of Troubles-Talk in Ordinary Conversation." *Social Problems* 35 (4): 418–441.
Jefferson, Gail, Harvey Sacks, and Emanuel A. Schegloff. 1987. "Notes on Laughter in Pursuit of Intimacy." In *Talk and Social Organisation*, edited by Graham Button and John R. E. Lee, 152–205. Clevedon; Philadelphia, PA: Multilingual Matters.
Jun, Sun-Ah. 2005. "Korean Intonational Phonology and Prosodic Transcription." In *Prosodic Typology the Phonology of Intonation and Phrasing*, edited by Sun-Ah Jun, 201–229. Oxford: Oxford University Press.
Kim, K. H., and K. H. Suh. 1993. "The Korean Modal Marker *Keyss* as a Marker of Affect: An Interactional Perspective." In *Japanese/Korean Linguistics*, edited by P. K. Clancy, 2: 98–114. Stanford, CA: Center for Study of Language and Information, Stanford University.
———. 1994. "The Discourse Connective Nikka in Korean Conversation." In *Japanese/Korean Linguistics*, edited by Noriko Akatsuka, Shōichi Iwasaki, and Susan Strauss, 4: 83–99. Stanford, CA: Center for Study of Language and Information, Stanford University.
Koshik, Irene. 2003. "Wh-Questions Used as Challenges." *Discourse Studies* 5: 51–78.
———. 2005. *Beyond Rhetorical Questions: Assertive Questions in Everyday Interaction*. Amsterdam: Benjamins.
———. 2017. "Responses to Wh-Question Challenges." In *Enabling Human Conduct: Studies of Talk-in-Interaction in Honor of Emanuel A. Schegloff*, edited by Geoffrey Raymond, Gene H. Lerner, and John Heritage, 81–103. Amsterdam: John Benjamins Publishing.
Kowalski, Robin M. 2003. *Complaining, Teasing, and Other Annoying Behaviors*. New Haven: Yale University Press.
Kramsch, Clare. 1998. *Language and Culture*. Oxford: Oxford University Press.
Lee, Hyo-Sang. 1999. "A Discourse-Pragmatic Analysis of the Committal-Ci in Korean: A Synthetic Approach to the Form-Meaning Relation." *Journal of Pragmatics* 31 (2): 243–275.
Lee, Jin-Sook. 1999. "Analysis of Pragmatic Speech Styles Among Korean Learners of English: A Focus on Complaint-Apology Speech Act Sequences." Unpublished Doctoral Dissertation, Stanford University.
Mandelbaum, Jenny. 1987. "Couples Sharing Stories." *Communication Quarterly* 35 (2): 144–170.
———. 1993. "Assigning Responsibility in Conversational Storytelling: The Interactional Construction of Reality." *Text* 12: 247–266.
———. 2003. "Interactive Methods for Constructing Relationships." In *Studies in Language and Social Interaction: In Honor of Robert Hopper (Book, 2014) [WorldCat.Org]*, edited by P. Glenn, D. LeBaron, and Jenny Mandelbaum, 207–219. New Jersey: Lawrence Erlbaum. https://www.worldcat.org/title/studies-in-language-and-social-interaction-in-honor-of-robert-hopper/oclc/877844276&referer=brief_results.
Maynard, Douglas. 1985. "How Children Start Arguments." *Language in Society* 14 (1): 1–29.

McCarthy, Michael. 1991. *Discourse Analysis for Language Teachers.* Cambridge: Cambridge University Press.

Moon, Young-In. 1996. "Interlanguage Features of Korean EFL Learners in the Communicative Act of Complaining." Unpublished Doctoral Dissertation, Indiana University.

Murphy, Beth, and Joyce Neu. 1996. "My Grade's Too Low: The Speech Act Set of Complaining." In *Speech Acts Across Cultures: Challenges to Communication in a Second Language*, edited by Susan Gass and Joyce Neu. Berlin: Mouton de Gruyter.

Ochs, Elinor, Emanuel A. Schegloff, and Sandra Thompson, eds. 1996. *Interaction and Grammar.* Cambridge: Cambridge University Press.

Oh, Sun-Young. 2002. "Referring to People in Korean and English." Unpublished Doctoral Dissertation, UCLA.

Olshtain, Elite, and Liora Weinbach. 1987. "Complaints: A Study of Speech Act Behavior Among Native and Non-Native Speakers of Hebrew." In *The Pragmatic Perspective*, edited by Marcella Bertucelli-Papi and Jef Verschueren, 195–208. Amsterdam: John Benjamins.

Park, Yong-Yae.1999. "The Korean Connective Nuntey in Conversational Discourse." *Journal of Pragmatics* 31: 191–218.

Pomerantz, Anita. 1984. "Agreeing and Disagreeing with Assessments: Some Features of Preferred/Dispreferred Turn Shapes." In *Structures of Social Action: Studies in Conversation Analysis*, edited by J. M. Atkinson and J. Heritage, 57–101. Cambridge: Cambridge University Press.

———. 1986. "Extreme Case for Formulations: A Way of Legitimizing Claims." *Human Studies* 9: 219–229.

Raymond, Geoffrey, and John Heritage. 2006. "The Epistemics of Social Relations: Owning Grandchildren." *Language in Society* 35 (5): 677–706.

Robinson, Jeffrey D. 2004. "The Sequential Organization of 'Explicit' Apologies in Naturally Occurring English." *Research on Language & Social Interaction* 37 (3): 291–330.

Sacks, Harvey. 1972. "On the Analyzability of Stories by Children." In *Directions in Sociolinguistics: The Ethnography of Communication*, edited by John J. Gumperz and Dell Hymes, 325–345. New York: Holt, Rinehart and Winston.

———. 1992. *Lectures on Conversation.* Oxford: Blackwell.

Sacks, Harvey, Emanuel A. Schegloff, and Gail Jefferson. 1974. "A Simplest Systematics for the Organization of Turn-Taking for Conversation." *Language* 50 (4): 696–735.

Schegloff, Emanuel A. 1982. "Discourse as an Interactional Achievement: Some Uses of 'Uh Huh' and Other Things That Come Between Sentences." In *Analyzing Discourse: Text and Talk*, edited by Deborah Tannen, 71–93. Washington, DC: Georgetown University Press.

———. 1986. "The Routine as Achievement." *Human Studies* 9 (2–3): 111–151.

———. 1988. "Goffman and the Analysis of Conversation." In *Erving Goffman: Exploring the Interaction Order*, edited by Paul Drew and Anthony Wootton, 89–135. Cambridge: Polity Press.

———. 1991. "Reflections on Talk and Social Structure." In *Talk and Social Structure*, edited by Deirdre Boden and Don H. Zimmerman, 44–70. Berkeley: University of California Press.

———. 1992. "On Talk and Its Institutional Occasions." In *Talk at Work: Interaction in Institutional Settings*, edited by Paul Drew and John Heritage, 101–134. Cambridge: Cambridge University Press.

———. 2005. "On Complainability." *Social Problems* 52 (4): 449–476.

———. 2007. *Sequence Organization in Interaction: A Primer in Conversation Analysis*. Cambridge: Cambridge University Press.

Selting, Margret, and Elizabeth Couper-Kuhlen, eds. 2001. *Studies in Interactional Linguistics*. Amsterdam: John Benjamins Publishing Company. http://www.myilibrary.com?id=225453.

Sohn, Ho-min. 1999. *The Korean Language*. Cambridge: Cambridge University Press.

Sotirova, Nadezhda. 2018. "A Cry and an Outcry: Oplakvane (Complaining) as a Term for Communication Practice." *Journal of International and Intercultural Communication* 11 (4): 304–323. DOI: 10.1080/17513057.2018.1479439.

Stivers, Tanya, Lorenza Mondada, and Jakob Steensig. 2011. "Knowledge, Morality and Affiliation in Social Interaction." In *The Morality of Knowledge in Conversation*, edited by Tanya Stivers, Lorenza Mondada, and Jakob Steensig, 3–24. Cambridge: Cambridge University Press.

Suh, Kyung-Hee. 2004. "Interactional Functions of Way in Korean Conversation." *Sahoe Onohak [The Sociolinguistic Journal of Korea]* 12 (2): 181–204.

Wolfson, Nessa. 1983. *Perspectives: Sociolinguistics and TESOL*. Cambridge: Newbury House Publishers.

Young, Richard F. 2008. *Language and Interaction: An Advanced Resource Book*. London: Routledge.

Index

absence-based formulation of complainability, 8–11, 21–25
account, 65, 75, 77–80, 88, 90–91, 93–94, 118, 125, 128, 130, 133, 139–140, 142
adjacency pair, 52
affective stance, 32, 100, 105, 108
affiliative response, 100, 101, 105–106, 108–109
ai, 42–43, 74
aikwu, 15, 42–43, 71–72, 107–108
alignment, 100, 108
apology, 37, 70, 75–77, 79, 88
aywu, 11–12, 42–43, 71–72, 103, 105

CA. *See* Conversation Analysis
ccom. See com
challenge question, 91–92
cham na, 44–45
change-of-state token, 104, 108
com, 44–46, 56
complainability formulation, 8–21
complaining. *See* complaint
complaint: definition of, 1–2. *See also* direct complaint; indirect complaint
contesting, 22, 65, 83, 88, 91
continuer, 104, 106–107

Conversation Analysis (CA), 3, 5, 113
counter-complaint, 16, 34, 64–65, 70, 72–73, 75, 79, 82, 84–86, 95, 98, 119, 128
cultural reality, 147

declaratives in complaints, 47–49
diminutive form, 25–27
direct complaint, 1, 70, 75–100, 113, 120, 136, 146. *See also* complaint; indirect complaint
disagreement, 12, 22, 32, 55, 90, 98–100

ehywu, 43
empathetic stance, 102
empathic stance, 101
ethnomethodological perspective, 3, 78, 113
excessive event, 14–18, 21, 28–32
extreme case formulations, 22, 146
eykey, 13, 27–28, 40–41
eyi, 42–43

face-threatening act, 113, 120, 122, 146
formal complaint, 2, 4, 48–49, 84–85. *See also* complaint
formality, 4

156 Index

group identity, 112. *See also* social membership

hel, 43–44

imperatives in complaints, 47, 56–58
indirect complaint, 1, 69, 99–112, 146. *See also* complaint; direct complaint
insufficient event, 11–14, 21, 25–28
intensifying expressions, 22, 24, 28, 32, 38
interactional linguistic research, 2
interrogatives with question words in complaints, 47, 49–52

Korean Tones and Break Indices (K-ToBI), 60–61
K-ToBI. *See* Korean Tones and Break Indices

later upward intonation, 59–66, 80, 82–83, 98, 105, 109
laughter, 104–106, 108, 111

membership categorization, 122–123, 134. *See also* social membership

negative event, 9
nemwu, 14–15, 17
newsmark, 90–91
non-affiliative chuckle, 108
normative orientation, 37, 55, 85, 117, 139

phrases in complaints, 49
positive politeness, 120, 122

post-expansion, 95
prospective indexical, 124, 143n1

reprehensibility, 2, 21, 23, 80, 133. *See also* complainability formulation
request, 17, 56, 75, 80, 82, 88, 93, 98, 116, 124, 128, 146
response cry, 12–13, 27–28, 35, 40–46, 64, 69–74, 80, 82, 111, 127
rhetorical question, 28
reversed polarity question (RPQ), 50–53, 55, 83, 98
RPQ. *See* reversed polarity question

sequencing practices, 75
social identities, 2–3, 6, 112–114, 118, 120, 142, 145–146
social memberships, 2, 6, 112–114, 121–123
social organization, 2–3, 5–6, 113, 142
social relations, 2, 5–6, 120–122, 142
social solidarity, 105, 120–121
sociocultural norm, 1–2, 5, 37, 75, 79, 86
speech act theory, 3, 146
speech styles, 4, 28, 77

topic termination, 108
triggering event, 14, 41, 66, 69–71
tto, 34–37

unacceptable event, 18–21, 32–37

"yes/no" interrogatives in complaints, 47, 53–56

About the Author

Kyung-Eun Yoon is senior lecturer in the Department of Modern Languages, Linguistics and Intercultural Communication at the University of Maryland, Baltimore County. Her research interests are conversation analysis, discourse analysis, and language pedagogy, related to the Korean language and culture. She is the author of several book chapters and many articles appearing in journals such as *Journal of Pragmatics*, *Journal of Linguistics*, *Studies in Language*, and *Korean Language in America*.

www.ingramcontent.com/pod-product-compliance
Lightning Source LLC
Chambersburg PA
CBHW050909300426
44111CB00010B/1441